ROMANS

THOMAS NELSON AND SONS LTD
Parkside Works Edinburgh 9
36 Park Street London W1
312 Flinders Street Melbourne C1

302–304 Barclays Bank Building
Commissioner and Kruis Streets
Johannesburg

THOMAS NELSON AND SONS (CANADA) LTD
91–93 Wellington Street West   Toronto 1

THOMAS NELSON AND SONS
19 East 47th Street New York 17

SOCIÉTÉ FRANÇAISE D'ÉDITIONS NELSON
97 rue Monge Paris 5

Printed in Great Britain by Thomas Nelson and Sons Ltd, Edinburgh

ROMANS

BY MICHAEL GRANT
AND DON POTTINGER

THOMAS NELSON & SONS LTD

FOREWORD

By various methods, including many military *tours de force* of awe-inspiring competence, the Romans gained control of an enormous area of the world, from the Euphrates to the Tagus and from the Scottish lowlands to the Sahara. Conquest was followed by law : throughout half a millennium the Romans sought to harness and control their cosmopolitan state. Their experiences, triumphant and disastrous alike, provide unending food for thought to that great majority of the human race who are living among the problems of multinational commonwealths today.

In a passage of which the beauty is in itself sufficient argument for learning Latin, Virgil assured his fellow-countrymen that imperial government was their métier, and that they could leave the fine arts to others. Yet it was Rome's peace and patronage that provided Greek and Asian artists and architects with new and incomparable opportunities to extend their ancient heritages. And in one field of the spirit, Virgil's own field of literary genius, the Romans themselves excelled—thereby demanding sympathetic attention from the English, who have likewise led Europe less with their paint-brushes or building designs than with their pens. Since most of our greatest writers were never long forgetful of Latin models, we cannot, without knowing something of Rome, understand our background ; we cannot, that is to say, understand ourselves.

With growing racial intermixture and material prosperity, the austere virtues and crudities of the early Roman gave place to the less granitic qualities of the typical citizen of imperial times. Although his taste in amusements remained unspeakable, at least outside the arena the brutalities of his inherited institution of slavery were gradually mitigated. Here the guides were exceptionally humane readers of those later Greeks who had discarded the city-state ideas in favour of a general human brotherhood—perhaps realisable, as the Christians also came to find their aims partly realisable, within the framework of Rome's world state.

Films about ancient Rome, if sometimes sketchy about pedantic details such as the order of events, are highly coloured and theatrical. In this, at least, they are right. Although, for millions throughout the empire, life was humdrum or even tedious—and the reasons for this seem worth exploring in the twentieth century—startling things often happened, sometimes in rapid succession ; and their effects and implications have reverberated for two thousand years. The people in charge of events, too, though we have chosen our own medium for their representation here, were sometimes only too worthy of glorious Technicolour. Their mobile, emphatic, often violent features, denying all reductions of history to a depersonalised continuum, suggest why the Renaissance, in its desire to explore what human beings could achieve, found the answers in ancient Rome. And there many people fruitfully continued to find them, until the contemporaries of Gladstone made the strange mistake of seeing Rome as nothing more than an unoriginal version of Greece.

MICHAEL GRANT AND DON POTTINGER

CONTENTS

ROME AND ITALY

The First Arrivals   8
Latins : The Seven Hills   9
The Sabines   10
The Early Romans   11
The Etruscans   12
The Etruscans   13
The Republic   14
Families and Farmers   15
Class and Law   16
Expansion in Italy   17
The Samnites   18
Roman Military Power   19
Rome and its Allies   20

WORLD POWER

Against the Greeks   22
Against Carthage   23
Against Carthage   24
The First Great Writers   25
Towards Imperialism   26
The Rulers   27
Money-Making   28

CRISIS

Roman Democrats   30
Menaces Far and Near   31
Dictatorship   32
Between Dictators   33
Julius Caesar   34
Julius Caesar   35
Rich and Poor   36

Designs for Living   37
Cleopatra Fails   38

PEACE BUT AUGUSTUS

The First Emperor   40
Organising Genius   41
Prosperity   42
Beyond the Frontiers   43
Nationalised Religion   44
Virgil and Livy   45
Designs for Loving   46

IMPERIAL TRAGEDIES AND TRIUMPHS

Queer Caesars   48
While Rome Burned   49
Army and Empire   50
Civil War and After   51
Epigrams and Education   52
Conquest and Culture   53
The Great Embittered   54
The Noblest of Them All   55
The Golden Age   56
Searching for Excitement   57
The Army Comes First   58

FALL AND ETERNITY OF ROME

Chaos and Recovery   60
Refuge from this World   61
New Rome   62
Eternal Rome   63

PART ONE
1000 - 260 B.C.
ROME AND ITALY

THE ROMAN TOGA

EARLY ROMAN

REPUBLICAN AND IMPERIAL

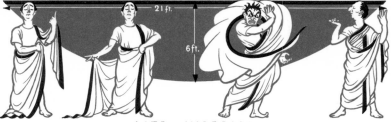

LATE IMPERIAL

At least three-quarters of Italy is hill country, dominated by the Apennines. These mountains divide the remaining flatter regions of the peninsula into four parts: the Po valley, indefensible and for a long time outside Italy; the long east coast, exposed, waterless, harbourless and sparsely populated; the warm, well-harboured maritime districts to the south; and the western shores, including fertile volcanic Campania with its three or four annual corn crops—and then, to its north-west, a coastal plain eighty miles wide, bisected by the River Tiber into

The Tiber was navigable by small ships

Latium is modern Campagna

Alban mount remained the religious centre (cult of Jupiter)

Earlier inhabitants of Latium: Palaeolithic traces, sparse Neolithic remains, some copper users

Etruria and Latium.

Above northern Latium rises a semi-circle of hills, dominated by Mt. Albano, fifteen miles from the sea and from Rome. Its volcanoes ceased to erupt *c.* 1000 B.C., after they had covered the earth with ash rich in phosphates and potash. When forests and scrub spread over the foothills, forming a surface soil containing nitrogenous matter, cultivation was profitable, and the Alban hills became the richest part of Latium. So groups of shepherd-farmers settled on these hills. Tradition made them settle Lavinium first and then Alba Longa (probably the modern Castel Gandolfo) but the latter is the higher of the two sites and may have been occupied first.

Then the immigrants began to move down into the plain of Latium. They found a rolling, scrub-covered upland landscape with steep, marshy valleys; a land of impermeable clay covered with fertile, porous, volcanic deposit (tufa), inclined to be swampy but yielding good harvests to laborious drainage even when partly submerged, and providing useful winter pasturage. This was the challenge which Rome had to meet.

LATINS: THE SEVEN HILLS

When these migrants came to the Tiber valley, fifteen miles from its mouth they found a deep trough ½ to 1½ miles wide, divided on its left bank into steep sloping hills, cut off by tributaries—now vanished—from each other and from the flat-topped spurs of the main hinterland.

Rome's Seven Hills : two on Palatine (Palatium, Cermalus), three on Esquiline (Fagutal, Oppius, Cispius), Velia (isthmus), Caelius

The legendary Aeneas, wandering after the sack of Troy, was said to have been hospitably received by the king of the Latins

JANICULUM HILL — CAMPUS MARTIUS — CAPITOLINE — QUIRINAL — VIMINAL — CERMALUS — PALATIUM — PALATINE HILL — VELIAN ISTHMUS — FAGUTAL — OPPIUS — CISPIUS — ESQUILINE — AVENTINE HILL — CAELIAN HILL

London too is at the lowest crossing before the river mouth

Perhaps caves on the Aventine had already been used as shelters

This place, the site of Rome, attracted the newcomers because it was well watered, pastured and protected, was situated midway between plain and hills, and commanded a possible river-crossing —the natural trackway from Etruria to the south. They settled on the hill that was most impregnable and nearest the river, the wooded, two-crested Palatine, with steep cliffs on three sides. Here (*c.* 800 B.C.) they constructed almost round or elliptical huts of reeds and twigs plastered with clay. The holes cut in the rock for their timber uprights and drainage channels can still be seen. The settlers expanded across the hill's one approach, the Velian isthmus, to the inner slopes of the Esquiline. Before long, when a village on the Caelian Hill made common cause, the "seven hills" were united.

These people were the Latins, a lowland race possessing a knowledge of iron, speaking an Indo-European tongue, and cremating their dead. Their forty or sixty tribes, loosely combined in a religious league, were the descendants of men who had crossed the Alps before 1000 B.C. and spread down eastern Italy, but had been diverted westwards by pressure from other peoples. They gradually changed from semi-nomadic herdsmen into agriculturalists cultivating wheat, millet, the vine and, later on, barley.

They kept the ashes of their dead in urns shaped like their huts

Very soon the ashes of their cremations appear in the swampy trough to the north of the Palatine Hill—the future Forum.

⟨ c. 800 B.C. ⟩

Shortly after these first cremations in the Forum, bodies of the dead were also buried there. They were buried by another race, the Sabines, belonging to a second great group of Italian peoples who occupied a large area of central Italy. These peoples, the Umbro-Sabellians, were of uncertain and probably mixed origin, but resembled the Latins in social organisation and religious outlook, and spoke Indo-European tongues like them—though their language contained strong alien elements, and they said "p" where the Latins used "q". The Umbro-Sabellians lived in villages perched on Apennine hill-tops, and their outliers, the Sabines, dwelt in the hills north-east of Rome. From there they came to live in Rome itself on the flat-spurred slopes of the Esquiline and Quirinal Hills. So they buried their dead in the adjoining Forum, where their Latin neighbours on the Palatine deposited their cremation urns.

Pod &
Quod

Latin "quod", Umbro-Sabellian (Oscan, Samnite, Umbrian) "pod": cf. in Celtic Goidelic "q", Brythonic "p"

Neolithic peoples had buried their dead

It was convenient for these two peoples to share the pasturage of their flocks. Meeting on the Esquiline, they gradually and perhaps peaceably united, and the product of their union was Rome. The Forum was drained and included in the city (c. 600–575), and the precipitous Capitoline Hill was converted into a citadel.

In the legend, two kings ruled together, Romulus the Latin (from "Roma") and Tatius ("daddy") the Sabine

Patriotic Latin myth: "Rape of the Sabine Women" who were carried off to Rome

Drain: the "Cloaca Maxima"

The pasture-land on the river became an important market for cattle—the basis of economy and the cause of wars. Rome asserted its claim to the salt deposits at the Tiber mouth and the salt route to central Italy, and the first wooden bridge was constructed, leading to the heart of the town and carrying much trade between Etruria and Campania. Rome was rapidly becoming an important centre.

To protect the crossing a fort was established across the river on Janiculum Hill

Salt was important to early peoples for preserving meat

*Senex =
an old man*

The early Romans, under their autocratic kings advised by a Senate (elders) and by priests, were acutely aware of something superhuman, beyond the common processes of nature, manifesting itself in stones, streams, caves, trees or exceptional persons. The most ancient places of worship were groves, from which voices seemed to come. Magic, the art of compelling nature, gradually gave place to religion, the art of persuading it. But many taboos dating from early times remained permanently, and the omens from the behaviour of birds, lightning and thunder continued to be watched as indications of future luck—good or bad.

A sort of personal identity was gradually attributed to Jupiter, the sky-power of the Italic peoples, arbiter of sun and rain. The other great divinities of earliest Rome were Mars, patron of war and agriculture—high god of the Latins—-and the Sabine deity Quirinus. Also potent were the Lares who guarded the house and land, the Penates who watched over the grain-store, Vesta the fire in every hut (and in her hut-like round temple), and Janus the door through whose arch outgoing armies marched. There were also many other gods, partly of Italian origin and partly borrowed or adapted from the Greeks.

*Jupiter the
Greek Zeus,
Mars the
Greek Ares,
Vesta the
Greek Hestia*

Roman religion had no mythology of its own. It was a conservative, unemotional, durable affair of meticulous ritual, prayerful sacrifice, purification, atonement and divination. These rites were largely taken over by the state, which bargained with the gods. For there had to be reciprocal service between human beings and superhuman powers : the "peace of the gods" would be preserved if man carried out his ritual duties. Associated with the strong native Roman morality, this concept of obligations gradually extended from ritual to conduct in general.

⟨ **800–550 B.C.** ⟩

Wall paintings from Etruscan tombs

The expansion of Rome was blocked, and then its development enriched and accelerated, by one of the great civilisations of the ancient world, that of the Etruscans. The country of plain, hills and dense forests beyond the Tiber's right bank contained their loosely federated city states, later twelve in number.

Gold fibula from Etruscan tomb

Their elaborate, individual art excelled in filigreed, granulated jewellery. The revealed religion in which they believed was a fear-ridden, ritualistic business requiring vast cities of corridor- and chamber-tombs for the dead. They loved bloodthirsty Games, feasting and music. Their language —though its inscriptions are largely incomprehensible to us—was evidently non-Indo-European. Despite early Greek influences upon their culture, all these features suggest affinities with the East; with Asia Minor, Egypt and the Levant, Babylonia and Chaldaea. So it is usually believed, as in ancient times, that Etruscan development began with the immigration—under pressure from great migratory movements in the middle east—of at least a nucleus of orientals, who intermarried with the earlier populations of Etruria or reduced them to serfdom. The Etruscans become identifiable as a separate civilisation shortly before 700. Within two centuries their cities had replaced monarchies by republics. Their chief occupations were trade, industry, agriculture, and particularly piracy and war. They made great use of horses, introducing the chariot to Italy. Their strength came from their working of metals: the copper of Tuscany and the iron of Elba were perhaps what had tempted them to settle, and the whole of northern Etruria became a region of mining.

Etruscan winged god

Etruscan art shows inner tension, dynamic rhythm, indifference to exact anatomy

Rome's Trojan legend may mirror historic migrations from Asia Minor

Pharmacy, medicine, thermal baths, and dentistry flourished

Women were prominent in Etruscan life

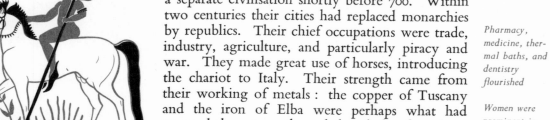

THE ETRUSCANS

Legend tells of
two Tarquins
(="king"), one
good (partly
Greek) and
one bad (ex-
pelled in favour
of Republic)

Juno and
Minerva
identified with
Greek Hera and
Athena

In the sixth century B.C. the Etruscan city-states rose to the climax of their power, dominating great regions of Italy from the Po valley to Campania. During this period, not long after the Latin-Sabine union, an Etruscan dynasty conquered and ruled Rome, making it the most prosperous city in the whole region. In c. 575–550 there were earthworks round the city, a pavement on the Forum, and a sudden transformation from primitive huts to monumental urban architecture. Upon the Capitoline Hill, beside the citadel, the Etruscans designed and built in stone upon a huge platform the largest temple in Italy, dedicated to Jupiter the Best and Greatest, Juno the ancient Italian goddess of women, and Minerva, patroness of handicrafts.

Though never truly a city of the Etruscans, Rome owed to their few dominant families its name and much of its government, religion, town-planning, technology and ceremonial. In alliance with a great maritime power in north Africa, Phoenician Tyre's colony Carthage, the Etruscans came into conflict with the Greeks, who during the two previous centuries had planted settlements on the coasts of the central as well as the eastern Mediterranean. Though the Greek colonisers of Massilia (Marseille) were defeated at sea by Carthaginians and Etruscans off Corsica (c. 535), the Etruscans were checked during the next sixty years by Greek Cumae in Campania and its Latin, Italian and Sicilian Greek allies. During this general decline of their power in central Italy the monarchy of the Etruscans at Rome was ousted (? c. 509).

Cumae was a
potent Hellen-
ising influence
upon Rome

Greco-Etrus-
can artistic
contacts were
now cut

Roman myth of
Horatius' de-
fence of Tiber
bridge against
Etruscans

Did Lars Por-
sena of Clusium
(see Macaulay's
Lays) recapture
Rome for a
time ?

Perhaps such a border fortress as Rome had changed hands more than once. Its final loss meant the end of Etruscan control over Latium and of their direct overland communications with Campania.

THE REPUBLIC

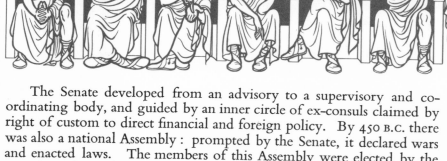

Senatus Popu-lusQue Ro-manus = the Senate and people of Rome

The departure of the kings was followed by the establishment of Republican government, under two annually elected consuls as the chief civil and military officials and magistrates. In an emergency it was possible to appoint a supreme dictator for six months. Their short-term, shared powers, and the diversion of the king's religious duties to others—a chief priest and a "king of the rites"—seemed adequate safeguards against tyranny.

Junior mem-bers rarely spoke

Male adult population under 60 was perhaps 25,000 (6th cent.). Voting by groups was a check on herd impulse

The three original tribes, based on kinship, would have excluded immigrants

The Senate developed from an advisory to a supervisory and co-ordinating body, and guided by an inner circle of ex-consuls claimed by right of custom to direct financial and foreign policy. By 450 B.C. there was also a national Assembly : prompted by the Senate, it declared wars and enacted laws. The members of this Assembly were elected by the consuls, and voted by groups of 100 men (centuries). The citizen body was further divided into five classes graded according to equipment. Thus the early Republic completed the process, perhaps begun under the later kings, of re-classifying the Roman people (after census) on a basis of wealth and age to meet the growing military needs of the day. Another change was the creation, on a geographical basis, of four urban and sixteen rustic "tribes", so that immigrants attracted to Rome by trade could readily be absorbed into liability for military service.

Class I provided all their own equipment, Class V only slings and stones
Front fighters formed phalanx

Cincinnatus was sum-moned to battle from his plough

The constitution looks unmethodical, with many possibilities of deadlock. Yet, given a general spirit of goodwill and reluctance to push any principle to its logical conclusion, overlaps were harmonised by tradition-respecting adaptation into a fair compromise between political discipline and freedom. The average early Roman was a thrifty, patient, narrow farmer-soldier, dutifully accepting authority and more interested in efficiency and justice than in politics.

Centre of gravity lay not in legislature but in executive

FAMILIES AND FARMERS

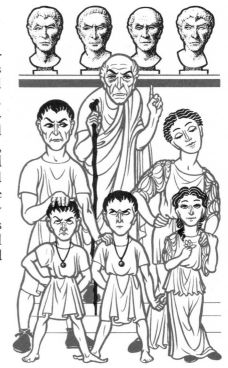

The basis of Roman society was the ancestor-venerating family, headed by the paterfamilias with patriarchal rigour only occasionally mitigated by his family council. Families were grouped in clans (*gentes*), each with a common name, religious observance and burial place. The original "patrician" clans (*c.* 500 B.C.)—Aemilii, Cornelii, Fabii, and two Sabine clans, the Claudii and Valerii—profited by the removal of the kings and soon wielded quasi-regal powers. Their sons, the "knights", led the battle on horseback, and every great man had increasingly numerous dependants (clients) to whom, prompted by hereditary moral and religious sanctions, he gave protection and land in exchange for support in his official career.

Clients helped to dower patron's daughters. Poor men without patrons lacked a safeguard

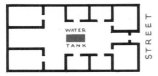

Basic plan
of a Roman house

Roof-tiles from c. 300 B.C.

Streets were narrow and dirty

Women were influential. In their wattle-and-daub huts—or, in more exalted circles, thatched houses of sun-dried bricks, eventually with stone foundations—they lived unsecluded lives, bringing up the children, weaving the family clothes, and managing the household. Though legally dependent on their husbands, they were allowed to own property and to attend chariot-races and military shows in the Circus Maximus. Divorce was easy but rare.

Diet : meal-porridge and vegetables

Early Roman treaties with Carthage and Massilia

Labour : ox, ass and farmer with hoe. (Fabii = "bean-men")

Rome though independent was now impoverished, with few outlets for exports. As cattle-pasturage had given way under Etruscan influence to cultivation, peasant-farmers (5–10 acres) had multiplied, but now the leading clans gradually increased their holdings to occupy the best of the land. Amid constant wars, there were severe famines, only ended by emergency state-purchases of grain from Cumae and Sicily. Grim debt laws made the debtor offer his own person as security, and a single bad season could reduce a citizen to slavery. So cries arose for the redistribution of public land. There were provisions for renting this from the state, but they were of little use without capital.

15

CLASS AND LAW

T he lower classes (plebeians), organising themselves to fight their rulers for better conditions, threatened and carried out protest withdrawals *en masse*. Before 450 they had compelled the government to recognise their protectors, the "tribunes of the people", who summoned the workers to meetings by their tribes and vetoed official acts against them.

Five secessions 494–287, some mythical

Probably ⅓ of this code (or of later versions) survives. Legal change possible by edict of city praetor (created 366)

Contact with foreigners added "law of nations". Greek ideas introduced philosophical element

Plebeian demands for a written law resulted in the appointment of a board of ten men (451–450) who produced a written code, the "Twelve Tables". This mixture of survivals and progressive ideas remained Rome's fundamental code and was the source of its outstanding achievement, the civil law. Roman law was precisely formulated in vigorous, terse Latin—a consistent body of doctrine rationally developed in a spirit of concrete, not unmerciful, equity. The Roman, at home in the law court as on the battlefield, believed in trial, evidence, proof, and the legal equality of free men. One early law, prominent in the Republican conception of liberty, prevented Romans from being executed without the Assembly's ratification.

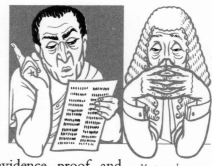

Most modern civil law (except in England) is based on Roman law

The next generation witnessed the rise of a middle-class army of heavy-armed infantry phalanxes (*c.* 430). The plebeians gained the right to inter-marry with the patricians. Then they secured admission to the consulship (366) and the censorship (351)—though this had been created, nearly a century earlier, to outbid them—and they also gradually increased their influence in the Assembly.

From 366 one consul had to be a plebeian. Censors registered citizens and property and (before 313) revised Senate-list

The first clear-cut personality in Roman history and its earliest prose-writer, Appius Claudius the Blind (censor 312), improved the voting power of the urban proletariat. Finally in *c.* 287 the resolutions of the plebeian meetings were given the force of law, and the people were sovereign. Nevertheless, what prevailed was neither the patrician nor the plebeian extremist faction, but a coalition between moderates on both sides. The protectors of the plebeians, the tribunes, henceforward placed their vetoes at the disposal of the Senate, which they attended and which, in an atmosphere of compromise, gained added responsibilities. Without any revolution, the Republican state had absorbed its dissident element.

Democracy was also checked by victorious wars and manipulation of religion

EXPANSION IN ITALY

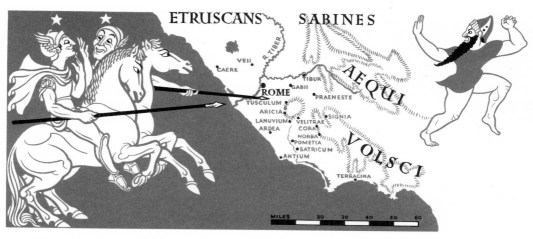

The Heavenly Twins Castor and Pollux were said to have intervened in the legendary Sabine defeat at the battle of Lake Regillus (c. 496)

Joining forces with its Latin neighbours, Rome defeated the Sabines (*c.* 449). But many years were needed (*c.* 498?–304) to wear down the Sabellian Volsci and Aequi—hill men to the east and south-east who coveted Roman grain, vegetables, and fruits.

By 500 B.C. Celts were in Britain, Spain and most of France

After a setback (*c.* 477) Rome's conquest of its wealthy and artistic Etruscan neighbour Veii, only 15 miles away (396), led to annexations which made it the largest state in Latium : a century of warfare had doubled Roman territory. Veii fell because the Etruscans failed to stand together. They were also weakened by the influx into Italy of hordes of savage, hard-riding Celtic Gauls belonging to a nation ultimately derived from the upper Danube basin. In these centuries successive waves of Gauls burst into and beyond the Po valley). One such marauding band disastrously defeated Rome's largest army to date on the River Allia, 11 miles north of Rome (*c.* 390). The city suffered a brief enemy occupation until the nomad Gauls, after they had committed serious destruction, were bought off. But from their base in northern Italy (Cisalpine Gaul), where they captured Bononia (Bologna), the Gauls continued to make raids.

The Gauls burst in on the Senate in session

Rome had earlier founded temple of Diana, in rivalry to their shrine on Lake Nemorensis (Nemi)

Anarchy after the Gaulish invasion caused the Latin League (700 sq. m.) to assert itself against the humiliated Romans. Relations seriously deteriorated when Rome, by its annexation of Tusculum (*c.* 381), drove a wedge in the middle of the Latins. War (343–338) resulted in Rome's dissolution of the Latin League and incorporation of the smaller states, of which the larger were reduced to subject allies.

17

THE SAMNITES

*First War
(343–341) may
be mythical*

*All Samnites
born in a given
year had to
emigrate when
grown up
(Custom of the
Sacred Spring)*

*Defeated
Romans had
to pass under
yoke of
spears*

Rome's reduction of the Latins led it to covet the fertile Campanian plain which lay beyond. The result was conflict with one of the principal branches of the Umbro-Sabellian peoples, the Oscan-speaking Samnites, a primitive war-like race of peasants and crofters living in semi-isolated communities in valleys and on plateaux. The cantons in which they were loosely grouped elected a supreme commander (for one campaign) in time of war. The Samnites were dedicated to expansion since they suffered from the same pressures of population as the other mountain peoples which had likewise clashed with Rome.

The Second Samnite War resulted in twenty years of stiff fighting. The shattering defeat of 20,000 Romans and allies at the Caudine Forks

*Rome took
Etruscan Caere
and Tarquinii
(353–351) and
NW. and N.
Etruria (c.280)

Roman and
allied army
now c. 40,000
men*

*At Sentinum
(295) Decius
Mus dedicated
himself to the
Infernal Gods
and charged to
his death*

led to an Etruscan intervention against Rome, but in the end the Samnites were prevented from encircling Campania from the south. Then, in the Third Samnite War (298–290), the enemy, allied with invading Gauls, was broken by the steadiness of the legions.

Though still independent, the Samnites were exhausted and depopulated. Roman man-power on the other hand, on inner lines against divided enemies, could match any coalition.

Reigning supreme in southern and central Italy and now the greatest state in the whole peninsula, Rome was clearly a potential Mediterranean power. Its triumphs of aggression had been achieved by more than two centuries of almost incessant and often desperate warfare on several fronts, aided by skilful diplomacy. War was popular among the Romans, who knew that more food could only be gained for men and cattle by winning more land.

ROMAN MILITARY POWER

Duing the siege of Veii the Romans introduced army pay to compensate for the cost of armour and keep the yeoman soldiers in the field throughout the year. Gradually, the city-state militia turned into an army, and skill and experience became more important qualifications for soldiering than wealth.

The disaster at the hands of the Gauls showed that a formation of pikemen could be rushed by a mobile enemy, and, once broken, could not cope with sword thrusts. Greater elasticity, suitable for hill fighting, was introduced by replacing the unwieldy six-deep phalanx by three-deep maniples of 120 infantry (in two 60-man centuries) fighting in open order. Then, perhaps in the Samnite wars, a throwing javelin replaced the thrusting spear as the chief offensive weapon of the front lines.

There were two legions, each of 30 maniples ("bundles of straw"—their ensign)

THE LEGION

FRONT LINE, "HASTATI"

| 10TH MANIPLE | 9TH MANIPLE | 8TH MANIPLE | 7TH MANIPLE | 6TH MANIPLE | 5TH MANIPLE | 4TH MANIPLE | 3RD MANIPLE | 2ND MANIPLE | 1ST MANIPLE | = 1200 MEN |

SECOND LINE, "PRINCIPES"

| 10TH MANIPLE | 9TH MANIPLE | 8TH MANIPLE | 7TH MANIPLE | 6TH MANIPLE | 5TH MANIPLE | 4TH MANIPLE | 3RD MANIPLE | 2ND MANIPLE | 1ST MANIPLE | = 1200 MEN |

THIRD LINE, "TRIARII"

| 10TH MANIPLE | 9TH MANIPLE | 8TH MANIPLE | 7TH MANIPLE | 6TH MANIPLE | 5TH MANIPLE | 4TH MANIPLE | 3RD MANIPLE | 2ND MANIPLE | 1ST MANIPLE | = 600 MEN |

PLUS 1000 LIGHT-ARMED TROOPS, "VELITES" = 1000 MEN

= 4000 MEN

Cavalry were only scouts and flank guards, light infantry and slingers could not manoeuvre independently

THE MANIPLE

JUNIOR CENTURION — STANDARD BEARER · SENIOR CENTURION — STANDARD BEARER

60 MEN PER CENTURY { JUNIOR CENTURY · "CENTURIA POSTERIOR" | SENIOR CENTURY · "CENTURIA PRIOR" } **120** MEN PER MANIPLE

SECOND IN COMMAND "OPTIO" · "OPTIO" SECOND IN COMMAND

(only 60 men per maniple in the third line)

The Romans devoted methodical care to fighting and, always ready to learn from experience and from enemies, they maintained the strictest drill and discipline of any people in Italy. War was learnt in a hard school—usually after an initial disaster—by endurance, thoroughness, ruthlessness, unflinching self-confidence, cool-tempered (if amateur) leadership, and a constitutional inability to accept defeat.

Evolution of marching camps more than once saved armies

Roman roads usually flag-stones covered by rubble layer and concrete bed, metalled by flagstones, rammed gravel or concrete

Another consequence of the Gallic invasion was a new city wall (c. 378), and a further vital military asset consisted of all-weather roads. In about the fourth century the Via Latina was constructed to link the city with Latium's south-east borders ; and to reinforce claims to Campania Appius Claudius constructed the 132-mile Via Appia, Queen of Roads, to Capua (312–310). The next strand in what was to become a pan-Italian network was the Via Valeria, extending an ancient road, which linked Rome with Tibur (Tivoli), eastwards to the Fucine Lake.

"All roads lead to Rome"

⟨ **390–280 B.C.** ⟩

ROME AND ITS ALLIES

By 260 B.C. the Roman confederacy extended over 52,000 square miles, exceeding in size all contemporary Mediterranean empires except that of the Seleucids (in SW. Asia). Its membership took two forms. First, many central Italians from sea to sea (10,000 sq. m.) were incorporated into the Roman state as full citizens or half-citizens, whose local communities possessed self-government. Secondly, there was an elaborate system of bilateral or unilateral alliances with 120–150 Treaty States, including tribes, a few of the old Latin cities, and increasingly numerous new "Latin colonies" consisting of both Latin and Roman settlers, theoretically on a basis of equality. These fortresses, subject to Rome only in foreign policy, guarded and consolidated battle gains, prepared further advances and encircled the Samnites. The latter, like other mountain peoples, were largely left to their superseded feudal methods.

292,000 adult male citizens in 264 B.C.

25–30 Latin colonies by mid-3rd century (2,500–6,000 men in each): but wholly Roman colonies (300 families each) on coast at Ostia (338 B.C.), Antium, Tarracina

Roman citizens paid a direct capital tax assessed on means. Allies, however, were exempted from all direct taxation (though settlers on Roman land paid rent). Their main burden was military service; they provided just over half the total force of the confederacy. Nevertheless these peoples, except for a few Latins, had no voice in determining peace or war.

Latins settling in Rome acquired Roman citizenship and vice versa

What they gained was the Pax Romana—including quotas of war booty ostensibly in repayment of taxes. Rome did not touch local constitutions and rarely intervened by force. Its methods were non-interfering compromise, "divide and rule", and the allurement of increases in privilege for those who were prepared to co-operate. Of the federal formulae already tried by the Latins and Greeks no use was made, perhaps partly because of the difficult communications and diverse dialects. Yet, very gradually, the Latin tongue and Roman law tended toward a common culture.

Rome sent the allies some supervisory officials: and garrisons in war-time

This period in which the farmers of Rome and Latium created a unique commonwealth was later thought of as a golden, uncorrupted, formative period of national character.

CIVIS ROMANVS SVM

PART TWO
282~133 B.C.
WORLD POWER

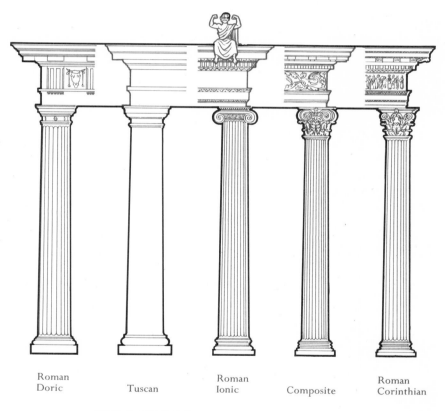

Roman
Doric

Tuscan

Roman
Ionic

Composite

Roman
Corinthian

THE "ORDERS" OF ROMAN ARCHITECTURE

AGAINST THE GREEKS

Italy and Greece had resumed relations in 4th century

Thurii was near the site of Sybaris, once famous for its luxury

Tarentum (of Spartan origin), rich in fisheries, purple-mussels and fruit, with fine gold coins, was first port of call from Greece

Rome's expansion into Southern Italy produced a clash with the most prosperous Greek city of the peninsula. This was Tarentum (Taranto), a moderate democracy—with a strong navy—which traded widely and manufactured clothes from the best fleeces in Italy. Rome was bound by treaty with Tarentum not to send warships into the Gulf of Otranto (? *c.* 303). However in 282 the Greek city of Thurii was hard pressed by native Lucanian tribes and appealed to Rome for help. When a Roman fleet entered Tarentine waters, war broke out.

"Pyrrhic victory"

Tarentum habitually relied on mercenary generals. It now sought help from the brilliant, chivalrous, opportunist half-Greek king of Epirus, Pyrrhus, who landed with 25,000 soldiers. He defeated the Romans in several battles, in which the projecting spearheads of his phalanx baffled the Roman infantry while his 20 elephants turned their flanks. Yet he lost more men than he could afford.

Phalanx as modified by Alexander the Great: like barbed wire

The great, luxurious, autocratically governed Corinthian colony of Syracuse, threatened by the Carthaginians' gradual domination of Sicily, sent him an appeal; and Pyrrhus moved to Sicily. He nearly, but not quite, succeeded in expelling the Carthaginians from the island, and then returned to Italy for a last brief encounter with the Romans. Finally Pyrrhus withdrew to Greece for a new attempt to conquer Macedonia. Two years later he was killed in a street fight.

Roman hero of the war: the poor but incorruptible Fabricius

The Romans had shown the Greek world the formidable power of their confederacy. They were now free to reduce the Italian Greeks to subject status, as part of a general consolidation of control throughout Italy.

Ptolemy II of Egypt became a Roman ally

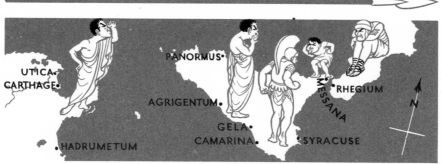

Rome and Carthage, renewing an ancient treaty, had recently (? *c.* 306) agreed to keep out of Sicily and Italy respectively. Italian coast towns were thus guaranteed against attacks from the Carthaginians, whose trade monopoly of the W. Mediterranean, however, was admitted. The hostility of Pyrrhus to both signatories resulted in an additional treaty between the two cities (279). But when the Carthaginians occupied Messana (Messina) on the Straits, Rome's Greek allies in S. Italy detected a threat to their safety and commerce. Messana appealed to Rome, and though the Senate hesitated the Assembly insisted on going to its help. So the First Punic War began.

" Regulus returned to captivity and death rather than advise peace" (? myth to justify his widow's cruelty to Carthaginian war-prisoners)

In an unexpected crisis both contestants had rushed in to secure a key position. With growing man-power, the political horizon and national aggressiveness of the Romans continued to expand, and as the war developed their aim became the conquest of all Sicily. Their Carthaginian enemies were wealthy commercial imperialists who, under a stable oligarchy, had extended their power from their N. African base (20,000 sq. m.) to Corsica, Sardinia, southern Spain and western Sicily.

Armies numbered 50–70,000. Total population of Roman confederacy 3 million, Carthage 5 million

This long and large-scale war (264–241) caused both sides tremendous losses. In spite of heavy defeats, including a disastrous invasion of Africa, victory went to the Romans. This was largely because of their enterprising decision to challenge Carthaginian naval supremacy by fleets equipped with boarding grapnels (crows). These immobilised enemy ships and enabled the soldiers to board and fight.

The Romans annexed Sicily, rich in corn, as their first overseas province, the kingdom of Syracuse being left independent. Faced with a serious rebellion among her mercenaries, Carthage had to hand over not only that island—and an indemnity—but Sardinia (another granary) and Corsica as well.

A carrier state: industry aimed at cheap mass production

Later Cicero praised the statecraft of 600-year long empire

Sea battles at Mycale (260), Ecnomus (256), Aegates Islands (241)

One Roman admiral dropped sacred chickens overboard when they refused to eat (bad omen): "Let them drink then"

⟨ **279–238 B.C.** ⟩

Hannibal's head on Spanish coin

At Cannae, containing and striking forces co-operated to encircle larger army

While Rome, under the democratic Gaius Flaminius, repelled a Gallic invasion—which reached Clusium (Chiusi) in 225—the imperialist Carthaginian house of Barca were seeking to compensate for their country's territorial, financial and human losses by conquering Spain as far north as the Ebro (237–219). Then Rome, probably prompted by its ancient ally Massilia (Marseille), attacked Saguntum (south of the Ebro), claiming that it was not, as it seemed, within Carthage's sphere of influence since it was of Greek origin and therefore separate.

Hamilcar, father of Hannibal, in Spain 237–228

But the twenty-seven-year-old general Hannibal, a military genius of impeccable and glamorous character, felt unable to endure further bullying. He struck back, and the Second Punic War (218–201) began with his bold Alpine crossing into Italy with 40,000 men, later raised to 80,000. He heavily defeated three Roman armies at Trebia (218), Trasimene (217), and finally Cannae (216), where Rome lost 25,000 dead and 10,000 prisoners. The city seemed at his mercy. Yet he failed to press home his victories against the exhaustion strategy of Fabius "the Delayer", the Senate's calmness, the people's unflinching morale, and Rome's superiority at sea and in man-power. Raising the legions to a total of 25, the Romans recovered disloyal Syracuse and Capua and retook Tarentum. Hasdrubal, bringing reinforcements from Spain to his brother Hannibal, was killed at Metaurus (207).

"Fabian Tactics"

But Rome's allies mostly remained loyal

Meanwhile Scipio Africanus was in Spain. Mystic and romantic—yet not far short of his enemy in offensive warfare, tactical reforms and strategic imagination—Scipio daringly swooped on New Carthage (Cartagena) and drove the Carthaginians out of Spain (209–206). Then he carried the war to Africa, where Hannibal, recalled from Italy after fifteen years, was finally defeated at Zama (202). Rome's resources had overcome his superior skill.

Scipio created a semi-professional army, and adopted the short, well-tempered, two-edged, cut-and-thrust Spanish sword

In nine years the Romans derived 130,000 lb. of silver and 4,000 lb. of gold from Spain

Although the invaders then evacuated Africa, Carthage was obliged to surrender her navy and agree to an indemnity payable in fifty annual instalments. For centuries, Rome was not seriously challenged again.

Spells against witchcraft, long chanted at harvest festivals and weddings, had been converted by the Romans on Greek models into crude dialogue, sung at performances by Etruscan professional dancers. This first approach to literary drama, which may be tentatively ascribed to the fourth century B.C., was followed by sketches with stock types. Then, after contacts with Greek culture, the Romans supplemented their Victory Games after the First Punic War (240) by staging Latin versions of Greek tragedies and perhaps comedies, written, produced, and acted by the Greek or half-Greek Livius Andronicus of Tarentum.

? first performance as expiatory ritual against plague

Old man, swindler, clown, glutton, were stock types in sketches from Atella (Campania)

But the first and greatest original Roman comic dramatist was Plautus of Sarsina (Mercato Saraceno in Umbria). During and after the Second Punic War he produced a varied series of plays "in Greek dress"—far more vigorous, racy and farcical than the Athenian New Comedy from which their themes were drawn. Adapting Greek metres to the different needs of Latin, he transformed the language into a vivid, pliant instrument. His great success was achieved in spite of temporary wooden stages, low and long, with auditoria of sloping soil; conventional dress, music and gestures; small casts doubling the parts; rival appeals to crude popular taste from boxing matches, chariot races and rope-dancing; and a vigilant official eye.

Comedies of humours and plot, romantic, domestic, burlesque and farce, ghost stories

Slaves wore red wigs, old men long white beards, perhaps masks

Meanwhile the poor but convivial "father of Roman poetry", Ennius of Rudiae in Calabria (239–169), enjoyed some patronage from Scipio. Ennius wrote Latin tragedies and comedies, satiric and philosophical poems, and a ruggedly grand first national epic much revered by later Romans—the *Annals*, of which 550 lines survive. The younger Scipio (Aemilianus) befriended the satiric poet Lucilius (*c.* 180–102) and the North African comic dramatist Terence (*c.* 195–159) who, writing for sophisticated audiences, developed the Plautine drama into plays containing fluent, graceful, well-constructed dialogues and soliloquies.

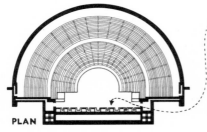

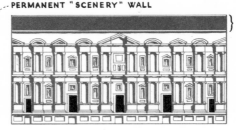

PERMANENT "SCENERY" WALL

Sloping roof over stage

Provincial Roman theatre 400 years later, built of stone, seating 7000

PLAN

⟨ 240–159 B.C. ⟩

TOWARDS IMPERIALISM

Flamininus

Rome was now drawn into the affairs of the large Greek states ruled by descendants of Alexander's generals : Macedonia, Egypt, the Seleucids and their offshoot in Asia Minor Pergamum, a kingdom of pro-Roman "traitors to Hellenism". By forming a protectorate against pirates on the E. Adriatic coast, the Romans irritated the ambitious, temperamental King Philip V of Macedonia. The subsequent clash (214–205) in which Philip was instigated by Carthage proved inconclusive. But then at the urging of Pergamum and Athens—still high in prestige—the Roman Senate persuaded the Assembly to reopen hostilities (200), and Flamininus, victor at Cynoscephalae in Thessaly (196), declared Greece "free".

Seleucid Asia Minor given to Pergamum and Rhodes (now leading city-state)

The idealistic Seleucid expansionist Antiochus III had harboured Hannibal, now a refugee from Carthage. By crossing into Europe, Antiochus aroused the alarm of the Romans who for the first time landed in Asia. The flexibility of the legions enabled them to defeat the much larger Seleucid army at Magnesia (Manisa, W. Asia Minor) in 189. There was now an imperialistic group in the Senate, and the Romans found permanent withdrawal from the Greek world impossible. Instead, at Pergamum's instigation, they attacked Philip's son Perseus—champion of the "oppressed democratic" Greeks—capturing him after the battle of Pydna (168). Macedonia, at first divided into four republics, was then absorbed by Rome (147). This was the first new province for over fifty years ; hitherto insufficient permanent officials, inadequate administrative organs and mistrust of distant commands had made the Romans reluctant to annex.

Macedonia and Spain (four wars 181–133) linked by roads to N. Italy

Illyricum annexed 167

Exploitation was increasing, governors more callous and corrupt

Cato : "Carthage must be destroyed". The site was ploughed over, sown with salt, and cursed

Now, however, the moral atmosphere was deteriorating. Losing patience with Greek quarrels and complexities, Rome plundered Corinth (146), dissolving the Achaean League which had given its Greek cities a certain power. In the same year, after a desperately fought three-year war instigated by Numidia, the younger Scipio (Aemilianus) stormed Carthage and converted its corn-producing hinterland into a new province of Africa. An even richer sixth province, Asia, was annexed (133) when the last monarch of Pergamum, as an insurance against social upheaval, bequeathed his kingdom to the Romans : they stamped out a revolution and took it over.

The sacker, Mummius, stipulated replacement for any Corinthian works of art lost on voyage to Rome. Roman soldiers were said to have diced on statues in transit

The Second Punic War, won by senatorial management, had checked for a century incipient moves towards a more democratic régime at Rome. The great families, combining with their traditional flair for politics and government a dangerous psychological combination of Mediterranean temperament and drive, maintained control over the elections as well as over finance and foreign policy. They succeeded by prestige, bribery, popular entertainments, armies of clients, and indefatigable marriage alliances. The system was to continue under the emperors.

cf. Peel :
"Damn the
Whigs, they
are all
cousins"

Among these arrogant, aggressive individualists there were no political parties. Amid fierce quarrels men gathered to their support whatever social and economic groups they could. On the whole, however, the ruggedly austere capitalist farmer-statesman Cato the Censor (d. 149) stood for conservatism. His opponent Scipio Aemilianus (d. 129)—a distinguished orator though not particularly forward-looking in politics—collected around himself men who, amid freedom of thought and discussion, attempted to blend the best elements of Greek and Roman life. His circle included not only Latin writers but the invaluable Greek historian of Rome, Polybius (c. 203–120) and the philosopher Panaetius. Panaetius retained the Stoic emphasis on morality but adapted its rigours to the careers of Roman statesmen by leaving room for imperfect "progression towards virtue".

Greek philosophers had earlier been expelled from Rome (173; 161).

There were now Greek tutors in wealthy homes

25 families provided 80% of the consuls from 200–146 B.C. Only 8 were from new families

The library of King Perseus was brought to Rome (167). Primary (3rd cent.) then secondary schools (literary courses) were instituted

There were also signs of a national Roman art, encouraged by Greek artistic currents percolating into the city. Generals had paintings of their victories carried in triumphal processions, candidates used pictorial propaganda in elections, and temples were decorated with mural paintings. The patrician families, which had from early times possessed the exclusive right to preserve death masks of their ancestors, displayed these at mid-second-century funerals.

MONEY-MAKING

The control exercised by the Senate was limited by one result of the wars, the rise of an important financial class. These were the "knights", originally young nobles but now all who reached a certain standard of wealth—second only to that of the senators, from whose career the knights remained apart. Senators were not supposed to engage in finance or trading, though they did so indirectly. But the knights controlled numerous financial agents known as "publicani". At first collectors of taxes, these publicani were entrusted —from the Second Punic War onwards—with state contracts (for construction work : roads, bridges, aqueducts), the provision of food for the army, and the operation of mines and fisheries. Mediterranean annexations gave them a fertile field of activity, and a number of joint-stock companies were formed. Though friction with elements in the Senate over policy control became evident from *c.* 169, other senators encouraged the knights who became active in money-lending, banking and trading. They were also allowed to help the state exploit its extensive property by collecting Italian tithes, grazing taxes and harbour dues.

This financial activity was assisted by the creation of a national coinage (*c.* 269) which in due course evolved its permanent silver unit the "denarius" (? *c.* 216). Perhaps first issued in South Italy, and adjusted to a Greek monetary standard, these "denarii" accompanied by bronze coins were soon minted in great quantities at Rome and elsewhere. During the first half of the second century indemnities, booty and mines doubled or trebled the wealth of the community. Rome itself was transformed by new temples of Greek marble, bridges, quays, larger houses (with Greek bathrooms) and tenements. Private pockets were filled—with a consequent decay of the old simple morality.

ROME
c.150 B.C.
▪▪.....TEMPLES

PART THREE

133 - 30 B.C.

CRISIS

After the wars, small-holdings on the old mainly subsistence basis had gradually diminished in favour of huge cash-crop ranches. The absentee capitalist landlords of these ranches found that land was the safest investment and that grazing paid better than growing corn. Such estates were increasingly staffed by numerous slaves provided by the wars. Their brutal ill-treatment provoked savage outbreaks by gangs of slave-deserters in Italy, and in Sicily 70,000 slaves under the Syrian Eunus temporarily seized several towns (135–132).

75,000 slaves from First Punic War, 30,000 at Tarentum alone (209). Asiatic supply from 189

Beef and mutton increasingly eaten by well-off Romans

Slaves as well as nationalists resisted Rome's annexation of Asia

The large estates also dispossessed the free poor, who drifted to the cities, unemployed, starving and violent. The high-minded young nobleman Tiberius Sempronius Gracchus, bringing his long-docile office of tribune

During his struggle with the Senate, Tiberius Gracchus wore mourning, appealing for protection for his wife and children, and employed a bodyguard of 3,000 men

back into revolutionary prominence (133), proposed to the Assembly that land occupied—at present precariously—by the state's tenants should be confirmed but limited and the surplus rented to the landless poor. He secured the deposition of a hostile fellow-tribune, but when in defiance of custom he stood for immediate re-election, he and 300 supporters were killed. A century of political violence had begun.

Gracchi: belief in the need for healthy peasantry plus the Greek idea of popular sovereignty

His more forcible and influential though not much more worldly-wise brother, Gaius, tribune in 123 and again in 122, proposed novel trading colonies (Tarentum, Carthage) and a limitation of rocketing corn prices. He also revived Tiberius's land laws. But this alarmed the members of the Italian confederacy who, increasingly ill-treated by Rome, feared the loss of their lands. So Gaius offered full Roman citizenship to all Latins and half-citizenship to other Italians. He also sowed future dissensions between Senate and knights by tempting the knights with the lucrative tax-farming of recently acquired Asia, and with admission to judgeships. Yet no class liked the favours to the others, so in 121 Gaius found himself a private citizen. A brawl led to the first emergency decree the Senate had ever passed, and in heavy fighting and the repression that ensued Gaius and 3000 others fell.

Senators on trial for corrupt governorships had been tried (since 149) by their fellow-members

Tax-farmers guaranteed the state a sum and took the balance.

But temporising agrarian laws followed

MENACES FAR AND NEAR

When Jugurtha, king of semi-dependent Numidia (N. Africa), offended the knights by allowing Italian traders to be killed (112), the Senate reluctantly declared war. They gave the command to Quintus Metellus, of the now dominant clan of the Caecilii. Metellus fought two promising campaigns, but his tough, sly subordinate and protégé Marius, intriguing against Metellus with the knights and masses at Rome, became consul and superseded him. Raising a part-volunteer army, Marius wore down Jugurtha, who was captured (105) and put to death.

Marius's election by the Assembly ignoring the Senate foreshadowed party struggles

Invasions and overpopulation had forced them (? ½ million persons) out of Jutland 15 years earlier. Rome had annexed S. Gaul (121) to protect Massilia against Gauls

Italy was now threatened by two huge German tribes on the trek, the Cimbri and Teutones, who humiliated several quarrelling amateur Roman generals, and at Arausio (Orange) destroyed 80,000 legionaries (105). But Marius, four times successively elected consul, although a "new man", annihilated the tribes in turn at Aquae Sextiae (Aix-en-Provence) (102) and Vercellae (101). A notable military innovator, he developed earlier experiments in the use of the cohort (600 men) as chief tactical unit. The now largely professional 10-cohort legions developed a formidable *esprit de corps*—and became more dependent on their generals than on the state.

"New man": with no consuls among his ancestors

At Aquae Sextiae 200,000 Germans were killed, rest mostly captured

In riots during Marius's sixth consulship (100), a tribune Saturninus, seeking to distribute state lands, was stoned to death. Disappointed beneficiaries flocked to Rome, but the government unwisely rebuffed them and expelled all non-Roman Italians from the city (95). When the spokesman of the confederates, Drusus, was obstructed and then murdered, they openly revolted, and the desperately fought Social or Marsian War followed. Some of Rome's Italian enemies were fighting to win Roman citizenship: others, notably the Samnites, to break Roman power. By resisting tenaciously and conceding the main issue at stake, Rome won. All men south of the Po became citizens, and those north of it acquired certain citizen rights (90–89).

Social War, from "socii" (allies): Marsians, warlike central Italian tribes

Confederate coin

DICTATORSHIP

Marius wanted the command against the charming, tortuous, murderous, half-Hellenised Iranian imperialist Mithradates of Pontus (N. Asia Minor). But the impoverished patrician Sulla had received the appointment, and after a sharp struggle in the streets of Rome Sulla asserted his claim by withdrawing to join his army and then (ominous precedent) marching on Rome. Marius armed slaves to support his cause but was outlawed and fled to Africa.

Sulla, who was perhaps the best Roman general since Scipio, left for the east and won back Greece from Mithradates. Meanwhile Marius, mentally unhinged, returned to the capital. After organising unprecedented massacres he died early in his seventh consulship (86), and his supporter Cinna (consul 87–84) was murdered. Their successors—backed by many Roman knights, Etruscans and Samnites—failed to prevent Sulla's return.

After three years of civil war and a blood-bath of thousands of his opponents, Sulla had himself made dictator (81)—but the original six-month time-limit of this office was waived pending the completion of national recovery.

Yet Sulla, brilliant, cruel, mystic and dissolute, did not intend to overthrow the traditional machinery of senatorial control. Backed by the aristocracy, he meant to make the system work. Liberally replenishing the decimated Senate from his supporters, he made office, in the official career, the sole qualification for future admission to its ranks.

He also tried to guard the Senate against future autocrats and subverters by limiting the duration of overseas commands, preventing recurrent consulships, tightening treason laws and discouraging tribunes—whose office he made a disqualification from all other posts. Sulla was also the first Roman to systematise the architecture of a large area of the city. At the age of 59, weary of war, power and Rome, and without aspiring to the final solution of lifelong rule, he announced an un-Roman abdication into private life. In retirement he hunted, wrote, drank with theatrical friends, and soon died. He was given a brilliant funeral.

When Mithradates overran Asia Minor 80,000 Italians were killed

Mithradates

Sulla killed 160,000 men in the east, leaving Asia Minor ruined

50,000 men on each side fell outside Rome (Sacriportus, Colline Gate). Political executions were organised by corps of ex-slaves

Age limit for senators was 30, consuls 42. The Senate was placed in sole charge of an expanded and improved criminal procedure

He built the Record Office linking Forum and Campus Martius

"No-one is rich who cannot keep an army on his income"
(Crassus)

The next years witnessed the rise of the affable, ambitious millionaire Crassus—patron of senators and knights—and the arrogant, shifty young Pompey. Both had won reputations fighting for Sulla, and Pompey had eliminated in Spain Marius's gallant supporter Sertorius (76–72). Subsequently Crassus had broken, and Pompey and finished off, 90,000 rebellious slaves under the Thracian gladiator Spartacus.

As consuls, each with an army behind him, Crassus and Pompey undermined Sulla's work by showing that the Senate could not control them. Then, against the Senate's wishes, the Assembly gave Pompey wide, un-Republican powers to deal with pirates in the eastern Mediterranean (67) and with the still unsuppressed Mithradates of Pontus.

Cicero had won a cause célèbre against a bad conservative governor, Verres (70)

By enormous bribery Caesar had become chief priest (63)

Pompey's appointment was supported by the "new man" and friend of the knights Cicero from Arpinum (b. 106), who had unequalled oratorical gifts ; and by the penurious aristocrat Caesar (b. 103 or 100). But in Pompey's absence Catiline, another blue-blooded pauper and an ex-tough of Sulla's, was disappointed for the consulship and turned to a programme of debt cancellation and then of armed revolution. Cicero, consul in 63, arrested six of Catiline's fellow-conspirators and had them executed. First, however, he received the backing of the Senate, led by the crafty, austerely principled Cato the Younger : Caesar, in opposition, advocated more moderate penalties. Early in the next year Catiline fell fighting against an army of the Republic near Pistoria (Pistoia).

Catiline was supported by displaced persons, debtor-land-owners and (at first only) by Crassus and Caesar

Pompey's settlement was the basis of subsequent Roman rule in the east

Pompey married Caesar's daughter Julia

Pompey was an outstanding commander with an instinct for amphibious warfare. In the east he achieved unprecedented successes, finally putting an end to Mithradates, annexing Seleucid Syria, and settling Judaea.

He returned without dictatorial intentions, but the ratification of his arrangements was blocked by the Senate—while Cicero talked only of his own successes. Thereupon Pompey, Caesar and Crassus united in the informal but irresistible First Triumvirate (60–59). Cicero's policy of "Harmony between the Orders" was frustrated, and the death throes of the Republic had begun.

⟨ 78–59 B.C. ⟩

JULIUS CAESAR

*Gauls gov-
erned by
nobles and
fanatical pro-
phet-priests
(Druids).
Metal-working
already highly
developed*

*Ships landed
between Dover
and Sandwich:
suffered
severely from
storms*

*Gallic cavalry
better than
Roman, but
infantry
undisciplined*

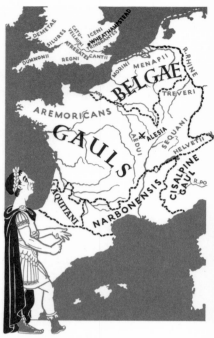

The division of spoils by the First Triumvirate gave Caesar the consulship (59) and a military command for five (later increased to ten) years in Illyricum and in Gaul on both sides of the Alps. Appeals from Celtic (Gaulish) chieftains against the Helvetii led him as far as the Rhine. Then he subjugated, often brutally, the disunited tribes of N. France and Belgium (58–57), and—operating by sea and land—the Atlantic seaboard (56). With the central tribes thus encircled, Caesar twice invaded Britain (55–54). He landed five legions (28 warships, 540 transports) and took the capital (Wheathampstead) of the strongest British chief and temporary generalissimo Cassivellaunus, but effected no conquests. Caesar was then confronted by a formidable coalition of central Gallic tribes. Beating off a large relieving army, he finally captured their leader Vercingetorix in 52 at Alesia (Alise-Ste-Reine). The newly conquered territory, of vast potential wealth, was constituted a province — "Long-haired Gaul".

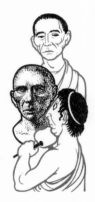

Meanwhile Cicero had been exiled to Greece (58–57) for his execution of the Catilinarians. When allowed to return he was powerless. Although subjected to many strains the Triumvirate was reaffirmed at Luca (Lucca) in 56. Pompey received the governorship of Spain for five years, but exercised it by proxy from Rome, surrounded by unprecedented grandeur and hordes of clients. He created a new monumental area centred upon his stone theatre in the Campus Martius (55). As Rome's population approached the million mark, public buildings were beginning to display revolutionary boldness in their arches and vaults, due to the rapidly improving use of concrete made from a local sandy earth (pozzolana) mixed with lime. Meanwhile the Roman portrait busts displayed in such public places began to show superb quality: their Greek artists were stimulated to achieve this by the metropolitan atmosphere and the individuality of their Roman models and patrons.

*Concrete
eliminated
"thrust" in
arches. Bricks
were added,
and lime-
stone and
marble facings*

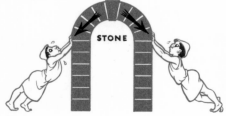

JULIUS CAESAR

ILLYRICUM

DALMATIA

CISALPINE GAUL

R.PO

R.RUBICON

ITALY

ROME

Crassus was killed at Carrhae (Haran) in 53 fighting against Rome's eastern neighbours the Parthians, and the Triumvirate was at an end. In 52 Pompey became sole consul (a precedent for emperors) amid increasing gang warfare. His wife, Caesar's daughter, had died and Pompey was pressed by senators into a breach with Caesar in order to limit the latter's tenure of his Gallic governorship and prevent him from becoming consul again. Whatever the constitutional rights and wrongs—and they are still disputed—the Republic crashed. A government designed for a modest city-state failed to prevent violence and corruption or control the commanders who could not be dispensed with in so huge an empire.

Caesar crossed the Rubicon (49) and occupied Italy, from which Pompey withdrew to the Balkans. There Caesar, after a rapid expedition to Spain, defeated him at Pharsalus (48), owing to the courage of his veterans in withstanding cavalry.

On landing in Egypt, Pompey was murdered. After a winter campaign there—alleviated by the company of the 22-year-old Cleopatra, confirmed as Queen—Caesar overwhelmed Mithradates' son Pharnaces at Zela in Asia Minor (47). Then he returned to Rome, and in further lightning wars crushed Pompey's sons in Africa in 46 (Thapsus—his strategic masterpiece) and in Spain in 45 (Munda—a grim soldiers' battle). No military innovator, Caesar possessed a startling sense of the moment to strike, a perfect comprehension of supply problems, and the supreme power of utilising and inspiring his unequalled legionaries.

Ruler of the whole Roman world, he caused the dictatorship, which he had held at intervals since 49, to be extended for life. A month later, amid grandiose building and veterans' commercial resettlement schemes and on the eve of an eastern expedition emulating Alexander, he was struck down by men who had enjoyed his favour or his pardon but could not endure autocracy. In spite of his clearness of vision, he had not yet attempted any far-reaching reforms of the state, which reverted to anarchy.

Feudal Iranian monarchy, Euphrates-Indus

Crassus succumbed to horse archer's "Parthian shot"

"I came, I saw, I conquered": Zela

He publicly rejected a royal diadem from Antony but was given, unofficially, many divine honours in his lifetime

Cleopatra bore him a son and followed him to Rome

Caesar: orator and lucid, concise, propagandist war-historian (Commentaries: Gallic War, Civil War)

Brutus, philosopher, and Cassius, man of action, killed Caesar beside Pompey's statue

Coin celebrating the murder, with cap of liberty

CRASSUS R.I.P.

POMPEY R.I.P.

EID MAR

⟨ 53–44 B.C. ⟩

RICH AND POOR

RICHER

POORER

? 120,000
settled by
Sulla, 80,000
by Caesar
(Corinth,
Carthage, etc.
colonised)

The Civil Wars caused great changes in the ownership of land. Through the influence of their generals, thousands of ex-soldiers were given allotments in Italy and the western provinces, but many found farming uncongenial. They and the evicted were often absorbed by the capitalist country estates. These new free tenants, who thus began to replace slave-labour, were mobilised by their powerful employers for political ends.

Though Mediterranean commerce was crippled by civil war and piracy, Italians formed active communities abroad. Provincial cities and client princes increasingly sought Roman-backed usurers, who charged enormous rates of interest.

Even Brutus charged 48% in Cyprus

In the capital 320,000 proletarians (Cicero's "dregs of Romulus") received free corn—yet the age of millionaires had begun. The richest of them, Crassus and Cicero's banker friend Atticus, lived modestly, but far more ostentatious display was now frequent. Upper-class houses were elaborately constructed, with libraries, parks, and statuary. Antique restrictions on senators' dinner plate were disregarded, and eating became increasingly complicated. For a change from metropolitan excitement there was the fashionable Bay of Naples, or Sabine or Alban mountain air ; while the city crowds were entertained by Triumphs and constantly extended public festivals.

Cicero, though always in debt, had 8 country mansions

Caesar exhibited 320 pairs of gladiators (65 B.C.) : as dictator he staged imitation naval battle

GARDEN

SEPARATE HOUSE

PILLARED

HOUSE

SHOP

SHOP

SHOP

WATER TANK

SHOP

COURT

SHOP

SHOP

OFFICE

BAKERY

SHOP

SHOP

STREET

SEE PAGE 15

The poet of this smart society was Catullus. Although a leading Latin representative of the movement of erudition, artistic perfectionism, and technical experiment which takes its name from Alexandria, he was as unswervingly direct as he was sophisticated. He wrote with poignant lyricism of his consuming love for "Lesbia". She was Clodia, the most notorious of the women who figured prominently in the social and, more or less behind the scenes, political life of Rome.

A writer of intense moods : the most personal poet of antiquity

The sister of aristocratic gang-leader Clodius—Cicero's enemy, killed in street-fight 52 B.C.

DESIGNS FOR LIVING

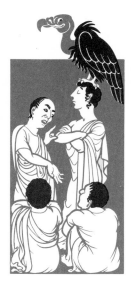

Imperturbability in all circumstances was a Stoic ideal

Within two years—before and after Caesar's death—Cicero produced an astonishing series of guides to living. They were popularisations, based on intelligent study and written in wonderful Latin, of the works of later Greek philosophical schools. Cicero particularly admired the Stoics, with their emphasis on morality and human co-operation, and the Academy (descended from Plato) under whose professors he studied, deriving from them a distaste for dogmatic creeds. By philosophical writing he consoled himself for his compulsory retirement and the death of his daughter Tullia. He also claimed the mission of providing the Romans with the best of Greek thought.

Cicero had joined Caesar's enemies but was pardoned

On Duties, Tusculan Disputations, On Old Age, On Friendship, etc.

The rival Epicurean case was stated with passionate eloquence in the hexameter poem of Lucretius (c. 94-55)

In the later 50s he had written more original syntheses, *On Laws* and *On the State*. In the latter, he envisaged an enlightened philosophical "leader" (? Pompey ? himself) for the already collapsing Republic. He also launched at that time his series of treatises explaining and extolling the duties of the orator. These duties take their place in a general humanistic theory of education—since no man was a true orator, in his opinion, unless he had an elevated character and well-trained, well-stocked mind.

Rhetoric was the basis of Roman higher education, recently instituted

58 speeches survive, ? 48 lost

Cicero's views on oratory were indeed authoritative owing to his unique success and persuasiveness in the courts. Though vacillating, extravagant and snobbish, on several occasions he stood up for his principles—which included a genuine distaste for soul-stultifying autocracy. So he struck bravely against the dictatorial aspirations of Antony in the outstandingly eloquent *Philippics* (44–43) which cost him his life.

12 Philippics, named after Demosthenes' attacks on Philip of Macedon

100 letters to Cicero also exist, but include none from Atticus

His extensively preserved writings include an incomparable collection of over 800 letters, many of them addressed to the non-political financier Atticus. These letters, together with his other works, comprise our principal source of information for the period, and because of them Cicero is the best-known figure of the ancient world.

⟨ 81–43 B.C. ⟩

CAESAR'S BOOTS

The Senate rallied against Antony's attempt to succeed to Caesar's power and defeated him in 43 at Mutina (Modena). But he then allied himself with the cold-bloodedly ambitious 20-year-old Octavian (the later Augustus)—adopted in his great-uncle Caesar's will as his son and principal heir. Joined by the light-weight Lepidus, who had succeeded Caesar as chief priest, they formed the Second Triumvirate—an officially constituted dictatorial committee to "reform the state" and avenge Caesar's murder. One of the many executed was Cicero. The triumvirs crushed the Republican cause at Philippi in Macedonia (42) and Brutus and Cassius committed suicide.

300 senators, 2,000 others killed

Antony was the real victor (Octavian, as often, was ill)

After the Treaty of Brundisium (Brindisi) in 40 between Antony and Octavian, the latter strengthened his hold on Italy and the western provinces. The surviving son of Pompey, Sextus, who had blockaded the peninsula, was eliminated in a naval battle off Naulochus in Sicily (36). Octavian then doubled his army by taking over the twenty-two legions of Lepidus who, though chief priest, was forced into seclusion. Meanwhile Antony had consolidated his control of the eastern provinces. Ignoring his wife Octavia (Octavian's sister) he bestowed the headship of an oriental hierarchy of princes upon the ambitious, intellectual Cleopatra—to whom, in his infatuation, he was suspected of sacrificing Roman interests.

"Queen of Kings, her sons"

Antony lost many Roman soldiers in a disastrous large-scale invasion of Parthian-controlled Armenia (36), whereas Octavian fought more successful campaigns in Illyricum and Dalmatia (35–34). Octavian induced the Senate to deprive Antony of his triumviral powers and to declare war on Cleopatra. She and Antony were decisively defeated in a naval battle off Actium in Epirus (31), in which Antony's crews, sapped by propaganda directed against his sybaritic oriental siren, failed to fight. Then they withdrew to Egypt where, as Octavian prepared the *coup de grâce*, both committed suicide (30). The Roman world was finally in the hands of a single man.

Each side shipped 35–40,000 legionaries

PART FOUR

30 B.C.- A.D. 14

PEACE
BUT AUGUSTUS

Allegory of Italy or Mother Earth, from the Altar of Peace (Ara Pacis), erected
B.C. 13–9 to celebrate the return of Augustus from Gaul and Spain.

THE FIRST EMPEROR

A ugustus—a name with antique religious associations by which the new autocrat chose to be called (27 B.C.)—maintained unchallengeable authority because he controlled the army and the empire's financial resources. Yet, describing his position by the term "princeps"—which lacked dictatorial trappings—and treating his powers as renewable, he revived and encouraged all the Republican forms and institutions. This publicity-enforced formula or fiction, despite a few sharply suppressed aristocratic conspirators, proved satisfactory to most Romans. Provided that there was peace, they were content with autocracy when it pretended to "restore the Republic".

The annexation of Egypt brought in extensive funds

Opposition literature did not survive : our sources are one-sided. But Augustus took pains to conciliate the nobility

By this iron hand in a velvet glove, Augustus influenced, indirectly, appointments to every important office. Chief among the friends whom he needed to help him in his vast task were the unfailingly competent Agrippa (d. 12 B.C.), almost co-regent, and the debauched, apparently indolent but watchful Etruscan literary patron Maecenas (d. 8 B.C.).

Although no emperor or ruling house ostensibly existed, Augustus aroused speculation about the succession by marrying his amusing, immoral daughter Julia first to a nephew Marcellus (d. 23 B.C.), then to Agrippa, and finally to his own stepson Tiberius. Augustus worked Tiberius even harder than his other helpers, but only reluctantly envisaged him as his successor (A.D. 4), after the premature deaths of the two sons of Agrippa and Julia.

Both Agrippa and Tiberius temporarily withdrew in pique

Julia banished for adultery 2 B.C.

Augustus, lucky in all else, unlucky in family deaths

Propaganda coin

Augustus was a simple-living small-townsman of literary tastes and skill ; the ingenious self-praise of his Acts survives on an Ankara temple. He combined a romantic admiration for Greek culture with an intense feeling for Rome and Italian tradition. But efficiency was what concerned him most, and he had a remarkable talent for it.

ORGANISING GENIUS

During his long reign Augustus took in hand all branches of the Roman administration and transformed them into an organism capable of bearing its imperial responsibilities. The principles which guided him were the primacy of Italy, the hierarchy of the Orders, and the suitable employment of able men. The Senate was purged but encouraged, under the leadership of the consuls, to undertake all its traditional duties "in collaboration with" the ruler. Moreover both he and they (at first informally) took on important new duties of jurisdiction, which gradually eclipsed the existing courts without replacing them.

City Prefect had troops under his command

Senior senators were chosen as members of new boards—controlling roads, aqueducts, public works—as well as for provincial governorships, in which the old amateur rascalities came to an end.

Extent of the Roman Empire in the time of Augustus

Africa and Asia were at the head of the "senatorial provinces", usually governed for only one year at a time. But Augustus himself "at the request of Senate and People" took over great regions of the empire, where most of the army was concentrated, as their supreme governor through "legates".

He effectively reorganised the Order of Knights so that its members should occupy the next-but-highest officer ranks in the army and provide the beginnings of an Imperial Civil Service, alongside the traditional system. Knights were posted in the provinces as "procurators" with financial duties including tax collection. They were also allowed as prizes the new Prefectures of Egypt, the Praetorian Guard (ruler's personal bodyguard), the Vigiles (fire-brigade and police force of 7,000 ex-slaves) and the Corn Supply—on the abundance of which his prestige depended.

"Imperial provinces" included Syria, Galatia, N. Spain, N. Gaul

Vast corn imports from N. Africa. One bad season would rocket prices. Free distribution to 200,000 in Rome

"publicani" retained for indirect taxes

The Guard later made and unmade emperors

⟨ 30 B.C.–A.D. 14 ⟩

PROSPERITY

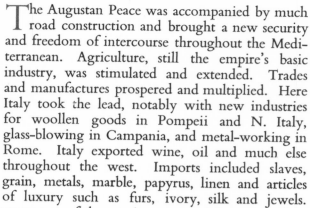

The Augustan Peace was accompanied by much road construction and brought a new security and freedom of intercourse throughout the Mediterranean. Agriculture, still the empire's basic industry, was stimulated and extended. Trades and manufactures prospered and multiplied. Here Italy took the lead, notably with new industries for woollen goods in Pompeii and N. Italy, glass-blowing in Campania, and metal-working in Rome. Italy exported wine, oil and much else throughout the west. Imports included slaves, grain, metals, marble, papyrus, linen and articles of luxury such as furs, ivory, silk and jewels. Though the internal commerce of the empire was more important than foreign trade, luxury goods had mainly to be fetched from abroad. Middlemen at Tashkurghan or Yarkand soon handled Chinese silk—for which a route avoiding Parthian intervention had to be kept open—and the journey to fetch Indian pepper and gems passed through Aden and benefited from Hippalus's discovery of the summer monsoon.

Customs duties were moderate, at flat rate (i.e. favouring propertied classes)

Syria and Asia Minor had great textile industries. Glass-blowing recently invented at Sidon (Phoenicia)

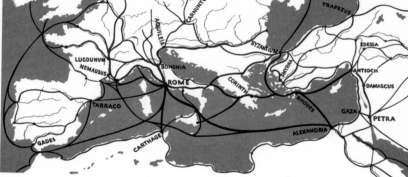

Main Trade Routes

The public had long disliked the old debased bronze coinage

Trade figured increasingly in official calculations of policy, but the state did not often actively intervene, except to influence and then control the principal mines. Spanish and other mines provided the metals for Augustus's new coinage. This was based on standard gold and silver denominations, upon which depended novel token currencies of acceptably bright yellow brass and red copper. These were the major components in a huge network of coinages including bronze issues by provincial governors and by scores of self-governing cities in east and west. This currency continued with minor modifications to serve the 50–70 million population of the empire—as well as conveying suitably inspired political messages far and wide by its inscriptions and designs.

Western mints included Lugdunum (Lyon), Nemausus (Nîmes), Caesaraugusta (Zaragoza)

Antioch, Alexandria were great mints as well as trading-centres. In Asia Minor 97 (later 312) cities coined

BEYOND THE FRONTIERS

Fighting with African peoples continued. Expedition to SW. Arabia (25–24 B.C.) failed

Provided that his own glory did not flag, Augustus preferred peaceful to warlike methods. Yet the reign saw much fighting—largely conducted by Agrippa and Augustus's stepsons Tiberius and Drusus—and consequent imperial expansion. The frontiers were pushed forward to include not only Egypt but a huge tract of Galatia in central Asia Minor, Numidia in N. Africa, the Danube borderlands from Switzerland to the Black Sea, Pannonia (Yugoslavia), and western and central Germany where the Elbe was reached in 9 B.C. The Elbe-Danube frontier, thus temporarily achieved, was shorter than the Rhine-Danube line.

300 ex-soldiers settled in Italy and overseas. Then pension scheme (A.D. 6) defrayed by death duty and sales tax

But the army was too economically fixed at 28 legions and 150,000 provincial auxiliaries, and the instability of territorial gains when no central reserve existed was shown by serious rebellions in Pannonia and then Germany (A.D. 6 and 9). The first of these prevented the conquest of Bohemia, and the second threw back the borders to the Rhine.

Arminius massacred Varus's three legions in Teutoburg Forest (A.D. 9)

PANNONIA (MAP ON P. 41)

GERMANY (QUAM CELERRIME)

Rome annexed Judaea in A.D. 6

Beyond many frontiers, and helping to guard them, was a *cordon sanitaire* of kingdoms under monarchs who, though officially independent, were "clients" of Augustus: notably Mauretania, the food-producing Bosporus (Crimea), the Nabataean Arabs (NW. Arabia), and their enemy Judaea—greatly developed by the Hellenised but murderous Herod the Great (43–4 B.C.). There were also countless princelings beyond the borders—in Germany, Britain and the Caucasus—who owed the emperor commercial or military allegiance in varying measures and nuances. A notorious bone of contention was still mountainous Armenia, which changed hands rapidly between puppets placed there by Rome and Parthia in turn. After a show of force by Tiberius, Augustus attempted a diplomatic settlement with Parthia (20 B.C.) and claimed that Armenia was now his, but it did not remain under his control.

Parthia handed over standards captured from Crassus

NATIONALISED RELIGION

Augustus utilised the traditional Roman religion to secure acceptance for his régime. This endeared him to many of the Italian upper and middle classes, among whom there was a vogue for antique, sometimes rustic, piety. The same policy provided effective consolation for the uneducated, whose religious feelings and superstitions had increasingly erupted into panic-stricken demonstrations roused by portents and prophecies. Amid ruinous civil wars, there had been widespread fear that relations with the divine powers had somehow been upset. This fear was calmed by Augustus's meticulous encouragement of ancient rites, restoration of crumbling temples and construction of splendid new ones such as the Palatine shrine of his radiant patron Apollo. Augustus's religious activity culminated in a magnificent celebration of the often-postponed Secular Games (17 B.C.), symbolising the purification of Rome from the pollutions of the past and the return of the long-awaited, Messianic Golden Age.

Gradually an innovation was introduced as the ruler, besides becoming chief priest on the death of Lepidus (12–11 B.C.), came to be accepted as a god.

Jesus was born in this reign, and crucified under Tiberius

The Games, for which Horace wrote a Hymn, had last been held in 146 B.C. (supposedly every 100-110 years)

"Maison Carrée,' Augustan temple, at Nemausus (Nîmes)

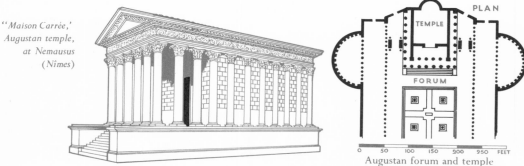

Augustan forum and temple

PLAN

TEMPLE

FORUM

0 50 100 150 200 250 FEET

This was in pursuance of the Hellenistic custom of ruler-worship based on grateful homage to the all-powerful God Made Manifest. The "Genius" of Augustus was added to shrines on the cross-roads—where its worship conducted by representatives of the local inhabitants was made official—and to Jupiter and the Penates (household gods) in oaths. His statues were placed with the standards in the legionary shrines. Then, finally, Tiberius dedicated an altar at Rome to the "numen", the more than human will, of Augustus (A.D. 13). In Italy, corporations—including ex-slaves—ministered to his worship, and elsewhere provincial committees and civic cults attained un-Roman heights or depths of adulation. Yet Augustus did not officially become a god of the Roman state (*divus*) until after his death. Those of his successors who died in favour achieved the same distinction.

cf. "genius" of paterfamilias in family cult

Temples of "Rome and Augustus" in Asia and Bithynia (29 B.C.), their altar built by 60 Gallic tribes (12 B.C.)

⟨ 30 B.C.–A.D. 14 ⟩

VIRGIL AND LIVY

Theocritus (3rd cent. B.C.) shows realism, the Eclogues (42–37) dreamlike unreality

"Messianic" Eclogue, ? for expected child of Octavian or Antony

Augustus had the good fortune and management to rally round himself Rome's greatest poets. Virgil, born near Mantua in 70 B.C., startled the literary world by the novelty of his ten short *Eclogues*, adapting for the Italian townsman with hauntingly evocative artistry the Greek pastoral themes of Theocritus. One poem, the fourth, cryptically prophesies the birth of a boy who will inaugurate the Golden Age.

The *Eclogues* were dedicated to Octavian (Augustus), and the *Georgics* (36–29 B.C.) to his and Virgil's friend Maecenas. In verse of a new, sensitive flexibility and power, the *Georgics* hymn the Roman homeland, the Italian countryside, the need for hard work, and the Augustan Peace.

Romantic epic : debts to Greek Apollonius Rhodius (3rd cent. B.C.)

Virgil was also master of the epic, but the subtle spirit of his romantic *Aeneid* is far removed from Homer's ballad-like extroversion, and so is the hitherto unthinkable rhythmical and musical elaboration of his poetry.

Aeneas escapes from captured Troy, and after many wanderings and adventures—including his tragic encounter with Dido—reaches Italy. Battles end in peace, Aeneas marries a Latin bride, and Rome's foundation will follow. For Virgil, enemies show nobility, wars turn to dust and ashes—yet he admired Augustus who had brought peace. The *Aeneid* was not quite finished at the time of Virgil's death in 19 B.C.

Livy : 59 B.C.– A.D. 17. 107 of his 142 books are lost

The same antiquarian love of Italy, and praise of Rome and Augustus, is evident in the moralising, emotional history of Livy of Patavium (Padua). Writing in rich, clear, strong prose, and making nobly imaginative—if by modern standards uncritical—use of many sources, his narratives of Rome's beginnings and heroic age and of Hannibal's invasion are masterpieces of dramatic art.

The half-mythical Camillus foreshadows Augustus. But Brutus and Cassius are respected

DESIGNS FOR LOVING

The youthful years of Horace of Venusia (65–8 B.C.) produced his bitter *Epodes*, and the *Satires* in which a Roman tradition was brought up to date in rapid, graceful, familiar hexameters with a humane, moralising tone. This tone achieved full maturity in the *Epistles*, the witty and charming products of a tasteful, gently philosophical and highly civilised mind.

With the Epistles is the Art of Poetry, pungent maxims for young writers

In his lyric *Odes*, poetic inspiration is modified by a calm, meticulous intellectual process and by his conviction that Augustus the peace-bringer was admirable : a belief he had in common with the otherwise profoundly different Virgil, whom he succeeded as "poet laureate". But whereas neither poet is servile, Horace is markedly detached and politely independent, with a keen sense of humour and surprise. These poems are written in astutely grouped, expressively compact Latin, ingeniously adapting Greek metres. They are about love, wine, nature, the gods, Horace's friends, Roman virtues, the transience of life and the folly of exaggeration.

Maecenas gave Horace his much-loved Sabine farm

Tibullus, elegist of love and peace, belonged to another literary circle, led by the soldier-statesman Messalla

This was also the epoch of the greatest Roman elegiac poets. A further protégé of Maecenas was the pale, slight, excitable Propertius of Asisium (Assisi). Veering quickly from ecstasy to depression, he wrote in poignant, morbid yet ironical terms about his disastrous affair with "Cynthia"—before turning, exhausted, to antiquarian national themes.

"The first young neurotic of European poetry"

Ovid of Sulmo (Sulmona) reacted against both personal feeling and patriotic morals. His rapid, dexterous, glittering verses look at men and especially women with sympathetic but clinical observation. Augustus the moralist exiled him for the remaining nine years of his life to Tomis (Constanţa) on the Black Sea, where he completed his elegiac Roman calendar (*Fasti*) and the 15-book *Metamorphoses*, an Arabian Nights of magic changes of shape displaying his narrative genius. Ovid also wrote laments on his exile—attributed to "a poem and a mistake".

Ovid's works include : Art and Cures of Love and On Painting the Face

PART FIVE
A.D. 14 ~ 235
IMPERIAL TRAGEDIES
AND TRIUMPHS

The Colosseum (Flavian Amphitheatre), mostly built A.D. 70–82, was the greatest
of all influences on Renaissance architects.

The next four reigns provide the long series of harrowing court melodramas described by Tacitus's *Annals* and Suetonius's *Lives*. Each emperor began with protestations of Republican and Augustan correctness, and then, under the pressure of his enormous power, degenerated to massive murders among the ruling class. Tiberius (A.D. 14–37) was an efficient provider of order, justice and economy, but was glum, misanthropic and intolerant of public relations and hypocrisy. Irked by his imperious mother Livia and hostility within his own family, he retired to Capri (A.D. 26) and ruled the empire through his Prefect of the Guard, Sejanus. But Sejanus, having removed Tiberius's heirs, was himself struck down, as prelude to a final holocaust of spyings, persecutions, vengeances and suicides.

Each emperor took the names Caesar and Augustus

Tiberius's grand-nephew Gaius "Caligula" (A.D. 37–41) emerged from an unhealthy upbringing and a serious illness as a fidgety, neurotic sadist. After his murder, the Guard secured the succession for his uncle Claudius (A.D. 41–54).

Caligula (= ''little boots'', in which he had appeared in camp as a baby) wished the Roman people had a single neck

Claudius stuttered, dribbled, dragged his feet, overate and overdrank

Imperial cabinet: Narcissus, Pallas, Callistus

Claudius was a man of learning and shrewdness, but of ridiculous appearance and behaviour. His reign was noteworthy for the extension of Roman citizenship in the provinces—in which the emperor, born at Lyon, was especially interested—and for the rapid development of an imperial civil service, led by ex-slaves enjoying unprecedented power and wealth. The members of this inner cabinet competed or co-operated with the emperor's third and fourth wives, the sexually unrestrained Messalina and the ruthlessly ambitious Agrippina the Younger. Agrippina poisoned Claudius and secured the succession for Nero, her own son by a former marriage.

New harbour built at Ostia. Arrangements made to indemnify shippers' losses at sea

The Pont du Gard, great aqueduct at Nîmes, was perhaps built about this time

Nero's head on coin

Nero drew, painted, modelled and wrote poetry. His eager participation in musical and dramatic contests scandalised the Senate. But his "bread and circuses" and personal appearances as a charioteer delighted the populace who were not offended by his self-indulgence and cruelty.

Begun under the good, if ineffective, influence of the philosopher Seneca and the Prefect of the Guard Burrus, his reign deteriorated when the horse-breeder Tigellinus succeeded as Prefect and chief adviser. To facilitate his marriage to the dazzling Poppaea, Nero caused the murders of his mother Agrippina and his high-minded wife Octavia. The Great Fire of Rome in 64 (probably accidental) was officially attributed to the Jewish sect of the Christians, whose first persecution now occurred. After the discovery of the conspiracy of Piso many of the ruling class were struck down. The emperor went on tour in Greece, but revolts broke out in Gaul and Spain. Nero, deserted by the army and Senate, fled from Rome and took his own life (A.D. 68).

St Peter and St Paul are believed to have died in these persecutions

Nero first sent his mother to sea in a special collapsible ship, but she survived

"What an artist perishes in me !" : Nero' last words. As a performer in Greece he won 1,800 crowns

Latin literature, second-rate since Augustus, experienced a revival in its "Silver Age". Although Stoic ideals were hard for a minister of Nero to live up to, Seneca's numerous treatises and nine tragedies are redolent of tolerance, clemency, humanity (including sympathy with slaves) and belief in Divine Providence. In a rhetorical variant of Seneca's scintillatingly epigrammatic style, his nephew Lucan—another friend of Nero—wrote the second greatest of Latin epics, the *Pharsalia*, on a historical subject, the war between Pompey and Caesar. Both Seneca and Lucan succumbed after Piso's plot. So did the epicure Petronius "the arbiter", who may be the author of the lively, scandalous, partly colloquial *Satyricon*—the first-known Latin novel, famous for the banquet of the coarse parvenu Trimalchio.

The plays of Seneca (born at Cordova) were for recitation, not the stage

Reconstruction after the fire, otherwise sensible, included Nero's Golden House

Wall-paintings included fantastic architectural perspectives

⟨ A.D. 54–68 ⟩

ARMY AND EMPIRE

Roman frontier post : watch-tower, ditch, earthen rampart, palisade, ditch beyond

Imperial scandals made little impact on the provinces, which amid improving material conditions and commercial development continued to be well governed. Tiberius, though a great commander, did not venture to leave Italy during his reign, and his successors—who were unfit to take the field—did not like entrusting commands to others. So warfare during these years was mainly defensive, and the army began to change from a field force into a border garrison.

Great troop concentrations near Rhine, Danube and Euphrates frontiers

Revolts due to abuses (e.g. in Gaul) were exceptional. "A good shepherd should shear but not flay his flock" (Tiberius)

However, the period opened with three years' expensive amphibious campaigning in Northern Germany under Tiberius's popular nephew Germanicus ; but the emperor recalled him before any annexations could be made. In the Danube lands Tiberius created a system of highways and Claudius opened up the Brenner and Great St Bernard routes across the Alps. In Africa prolonged fighting on the Sahara border under Tiberius was followed by the annexation of Mauretania. But Augustus had bequeathed advice not to extend the frontiers any farther, and usually this advice was respected. The exception was Britain, which the generals of Claudius annexed as far as the Severn and Trent (43–52). The emperor himself briefly took part in order to acquire a military reputation.

Boudicca (Boadicea) burnt London and Verulamium (61)

Tiberius annexed kingdoms in E. Asia Minor to strengthen frontier

In regard to the Armenian throne, Augustus's successors at first continued his policy of attempting to maintain Roman authority with the minimum military effort—in face of a strong Parthian monarch, Artabanus. Then Nero, nervous of campaigns by his publicity-minded general Corbulo, successfully arranged a long-lasting diplomatic solution by himself magnificently crowning Parthia's nominee Tiridates at Rome (A.D. 66).

Soldiers of Nero explored Upper Nile to S. Sudan and planned advance to Caspian

Coin of the Jewish rising

The chief area of disturbance was among the restless Jewish population of Palestine, where moderates and extremists joined in a national uprising which Vespasian had begun to put down at the time of Nero's death.

Jewish War narrated in Greek by Josephus

CIVIL WAR AND AFTER

The Year of the Four Emperors, theme of Tacitus's *Histories*, showed that emperors need not have Julian or Claudian blood, and that they could be appointed away from Rome—by the legions. The elderly aristocrat Galba led the Spanish army to Rome. But he seemed miserly to the jealous Praetorian Guard, who lynched him and proclaimed Otho (Jan. A.D. 69)—a man of fashion. Meanwhile, however, the legions on the German frontier had declared for one of their governors, Vitellius, whose generals successfully launched a two-pronged invasion of Italy. Otho committed suicide. Yet before the year was over the gluttonous Vitellius had also met his death, after defeat by the forces of the governor of Judaea, Vespasian.

Two battles near Cremona : Otho v. Vitellius (April), Vitellius v. Vespasian (Oct.)

Otho supported the memory of Nero, who had stolen his wife (Poppaea). Otho and Vitellius were of new imperial aristocracy

 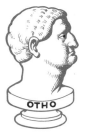     

GALBA OTHO VITELLIUS FLAVIANS / OTHERS VESPASIAN TITUS DOMITIAN

Titus had recaptured Jerusalem (70) : the Temple was burnt down and not rebuilt

Herculaneum, Pompeii and Stabiae buried in volcanic dust, much preserved—including 7,000 scrawls on walls

This sensibly frugal, bourgeois, not unhumorous Italian (69–79) founded a new (Flavian) dynasty. After suppressing a national Germano-Gallic revolt, he restored the ruined imperial finances, reorganised the army, and created a new aristocracy of provincial origin. Following the brief reign of his popular but prodigal son Titus—noteworthy for a catastrophic eruption of Vesuvius (80)—the latter's able, priggish, cruel, frustrated brother Domitian gave the principate a more frankly monarchical character. His high-handed measures incurred the hatred of the Senate, in whose ranks developed an opposition party, often supporting its Republicanism by philosophical slogans. The repression of such men turned into a reign of terror during the last years of Domitian, who was himself assassinated (96).

Nationalisation of mines and public lands completed. Important public works included Colosseum, on site of Nero's Golden House

House of the Vettii, Pompeii

GARDEN WATER TANK PLAN

In Asia Minor, Vespasian had united the central area and created a road system covering the frontier. The English lowlands were safe-guarded by the Scottish campaigns of Agricola, who defeated the momentarily combined Highland chiefs in 84. Similar protective advances carried the German frontier to the Neckar. Beyond the lower Danube, Domitian began to face a new danger from Decebalus, wealthy king of the Dacians (86–9).

⟨ A.D. 68–96 ⟩

EPIGRAMS AND EDUCATION

Political surveillance had a somewhat discouraging effect on literature. Poets active under Domitian, however, included Statius of Naples. One of several contemporary epic poets, he is now felt to be more noteworthy for the learned, smooth beauties of the shorter poems in his miscellany the *Silvae*. His Spanish contemporary Martial, witty, direct, humane, sometimes untranslatable—founder of the European epigram—cast vivid light upon the Roman scene.

Famous short poem To Sleep

Many of Martial's poems complain of the stinginess of patrons

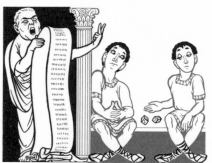

Martial's compatriot Quintilian (*c.* 35–95) became famous under Vespasian as advocate and teacher of rhetoric at Rome—the first to receive a salary from the state. After twenty years he retired to become tutor to Domitian's grand-nephews and to write his *Training of an Orator*. This is filled with acute, practical discussions of education in many of its aspects and contains a famous list, with brief comments, of Greek and Latin authors deserving study.

Quintilian: "supreme guide of wayward youth" (Martial)

Another writer enjoying close relations with the Flavian emperors was Pliny the Elder of Comum (Como). This man of extraordinary industry and encyclopaedic though uncritical knowledge wrote, among much else, a *Natural History* in 37 books.

Pliny the Elder's vast historical writings are lost

This work, which survives, contains a great deal of curious information and sturdy comment concerning the civilisation of the Romans. His death in the eruption of Vesuvius is vividly recorded by his nephew Pliny the Younger (*c.* 61–113). A pupil of Quintilian, the younger Pliny is notable for his nine charming, varied books of literary letters, and for a tenth containing correspondence which as governor of Bithynia, in Asia Minor, he exchanged with Trajan. These letters include inquiries and directives concerning the treatment of Christians, whom the emperor requested that those in office should punish if they were recalcitrant, without hunting them out.

Other Roman scientific writers mostly lost except Vitruvius (architecture); Celsus (medicine); Cato, Varro, Columella (agriculture)

Leniency or otherwise of this direction much disputed

After Domitian's assassination, the well-meaning, elderly Nerva (96–8) encountered trouble from the Praetorian Guard which had not been in the plot. So Nerva set a precedent to the next three rulers by adopting and designating as his successor the most competent man available—the great soldier Trajan (98–117), descendant of Roman settlers in Spain. In a series of major campaigns Trajan reduced and annexed Dacia, seizing important treasures and mines which, for once, more than paid for the wars. He also overran a large part of the Parthian empire, capturing its capital Ctesiphon (Kut) and sailing down the Tigris to the Persian Gulf. His campaigns were commemorated on a Column in the splendid new Forum of Trajan. Not only a conqueror, Trajan was kind and unassuming, devoting great care to the welfare of Italy and the provinces. He was acclaimed "best of rulers".

First non-Italian emperor —no doubt with Spanish blood

New provinces : Armenia, Mesopotamia, Arabia (NW.) (former client-state)

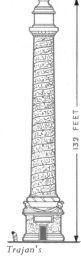

Trajan's Column

132 FEET

When Trajan died in Asia Minor, another Spaniard, Hadrian, succeeded him. This restless, extraordinarily versatile administrator, soldier, sight-seer, Hellenist and poet completed a reorganisation of the public service, separating the civilian from the military career. However, he spent more than half his reign traversing and benefiting the empire, throughout which he put into effect a new, provincial's conception of partnership between Rome and the provinces. His visit to Britain led to the construction of a Wall from Solway to Tyne (*c.* 122–9). On his accession Hadrian had evacuated the Mesopotamian and Armenian conquests of Trajan, whose rear had been threatened by widespread Jewish revolts ; these savagely recurred in Hadrian's last years.

Jewish revolt : Rome claimed destruction of 50 fortresses, 985 villages, 580,000 men

The 142-ft. dome of Hadrian's reconstruction of the Augustan Pantheon was a masterpiece of Rome's epoch-making vault construction

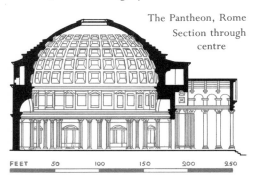

The Pantheon, Rome
Section through centre

FEET 50 100 150 200 250

Hadrian's Wall

Hadrian's Wall : 17 forts, 50 mile-castles (camps for signallers)

Salvius Julianus : outstanding jurist and codifier

Patron and practitioner of letters and architecture, Hadrian gave Rome a new Athenaeum, where poets and orators recited and lectures were given on philosophy, rhetoric and grammar. Law was also taught there, and developed remarkably under this emperor.

Agricola fought the Caledonians at the (unidentifiable) Mons Graupius

The historian Tacitus (*c.* A.D. 55–? *c.* 120), may have been the son of a revenue officer at Cologne or Trier. He was profoundly affected by the anxieties of office under Domitian, whom he criticised posthumously in a biography of his own father-in-law Agricola, governor of Britain. At about the same time as the *Agricola* (*c.* 98), Tacitus published an ethnographic, moralising treatise *Germania*. Then he turned to his life's work, the history of Rome from Tiberius to Domitian.

Famous speaker, believed to be author of thoughtful Dialogue on Orators

Of the *Histories* (on the years A.D. 68–96) only the first part, describing the Civil Wars, has survived, but we have most of the subsequently published *Annals*, dealing with the period 14–68. These outstanding works, written in an increasingly individual, enigmatic and vivid style, claim impartiality. But in spite of penetrating insight into character they betray a bias against the unforgettably portrayed Tiberius, who is seen as the forerunner of Domitian. Their absorbing, incisive narration, with its ethical trend, pinpoints the oppressive rather than the constructive aspects of the imperial régime. However, Tacitus notes that things are better under Trajan, and even in dealing with earlier and terrifying conditions he persists in believing that human nature, though liable to degeneration, is capable of great heroism.

Tacitus's immediate forerunners lost

Contemporary biographers : Suetonius (c. 69–140), vividly journalistic Latin ; Plutarch, comparative lives of Greeks and Romans (in Greek)

TIBERIUS

An equally searing view of Rome, despite current improvements, is presented by the satiric poet Juvenal of Aquinum (*c.* 50–after 127), who practised declamation until middle age and did not forget the relative poverty from which he had emerged. His attacks on the vices, abuses and follies of Roman life are famous for their bitter, pessimistic irony, crushing epigram and invective, hatred of women, and sympathy for the underdog. They contain grimly compelling pictures of the capital which contrast strangely with the genial accounts by his contemporary Pliny the Younger.

He discreetly relates many criticisms to long-past epochs of Tiberius or Nero. Perhaps banished by Domitian, he admits to "savage indignation"

⟨ c. A.D. 80–130 ⟩

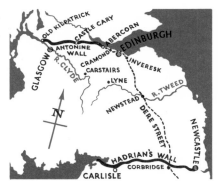

Antoninus Pius (138–61), descendant of immigrants from Gaul, had been adopted by Hadrian shortly before the latter's death.   During his peaceful reign this frugal, unbrilliant but devoted and tolerant ruler retreated from the cosmopolitanism of Hadrian and spent nearly all his time in Italy, where his centralised government was humane and painstaking. A minor expansion was attempted only in Britain, where revolts caused a new fortified line to be established between the Forth and Clyde (*c.* 142–3).

Antoninus called off Hadrian's campaign against the Jewish Law

This Antonine Wall was repeatedly assailed

At Hadrian's wish, Antoninus had adopted his nephew the young Marcus Aurelius (161–80) and Lucius Verus, and they reigned jointly, though Verus was a cipher. Aurelius, introvert and inclined to melancholy yet passionately conscientious, provided the noble spectacle of a Stoic philosopher ruling in accordance with his principles —which he has bequeathed to us, in Greek, by his *Meditations.*

Aurelius married Antoninus's beautiful daughter Faustina

Much Stoic thinking was incorporated into Christianity. Epictetus (c. 55–135) had adapted Stoicism to the poor

However, he had to spend nearly all his reign fighting. When Parthia forcibly reopened the Armenian question, Roman commanders destroyed its two principal cities, Seleucia and Ctesiphon, and a vassal state in west Mesopotamia changed hands. A more novel and ominous threat was provided by mass movements among the south German peoples, for at a time when the Roman empire was devastated by plague, the Marcomanni and the Quadi swept through the provinces into northern Italy (167). Raising funds by desperate means, Aurelius gradually drove them back and was intending to straighten the frontier by advancing it to the Carpathians and Bohemian mountains when he died. The German break-through, like the rebellions in the rear of Trajan's eastern operations, had confirmed that the Roman army, largely engaged in continuous frontier-patrols, lacked an adequate reserve.

He sold off the imperial wardrobe and jewels and debased the silver coinage

Except for most Praetorians, the soldiers were new provincials

THE GOLDEN AGE?

Diffusion of comforts: cf. 19th century

It has been maintained that no other period in the world's history has witnessed such widespread prosperity, comfort and happiness as the second century A.D. These blessings did not extend to the native proletariat of the provinces, yet they reached much farther than ever before. The emperors helped Italian municipalities to finance public-assistance schemes, and the lot even of slaves was through the humanity of state and philosophers substantially bettered.

Urban middle class gradually Hellenised and Romanised the empire

Though technical innovations lagged, general pacification and improved communications created larger-scale, decentralised industries, and fresh sources of raw materials were tapped. Gaul developed factories for pottery, glass and bronze goods, and the Rhineland became Europe's principal workshop. In the east, too, production and export trade increasingly flourished. Thus Italy began to lose its economic supremacy, though Rome with its expanded port of Ostia retained its preponderance in Mediterranean markets. There were millionaires in the provinces as well as in Italy, but this was chiefly an age of the wealthy bourgeois. With their support the traditional autonomous institutions flourished in thousands of cities—including many newly founded communities—-with elaborate and luxurious public buildings.

New goldfield in Dacia; iron and lead from Britain; ceramic industry successively at Gallic and Rhenish factories

There were many landowners living on rents

Population of Ostia now about 100,000 living in tall, well-lit, brick-built blocks. The harbour had been made safe for large ships

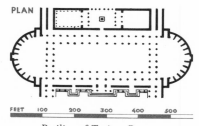

PLAN

Basilica of Trajan, Rome
Hall of justice
and commercial-exchange

New towns in Africa, Asia Minor, Levant: large areas in Syria wholly urbanised: many camps on Rhine and Danube became cities

Houses in Ostia

The favoured populace of Rome itself enjoyed ever-increased distributions of wine and oil, while the annual number of festival days rose to 130—twice the Republican total. All municipalities which could afford to followed suit. Meantime the educated classes, bilingual in Latin and Greek, flocked to the lectures of travelling philosophers, the "sophists". Some of these earned enormous fees: notably Herodes Atticus, a popular lecturer—made consul by Antoninus—who conferred lavish donations upon Greek cities. It was through such endowments of cultural foundations, and through the conditions of the Pax Romana in general, that the classical Greek writers could be preserved and studied.

Endowments included great libraries, e.g. 23,000 books presented to grandiose Timgad (Numidia)

SEARCHING FOR EXCITEMENT

Though politically calm, this was a time of spiritual restlessness and excitement. These feelings are reflected by the advocate, sophist and novelist Apuleius (born *c.* 123), the first of many remarkable literary figures to come from North Africa. Written in effervescent Latin, outrunning classical rules, his *Apologia* is a defence against charges of bewitchment, and his *Metamorphoses* ("Golden Ass") an eventful wondertale of a man transformed into a donkey.

Significant of the age—in contrast to Apuleius's nonchalant treatment of the Olympian gods—is his passionate eulogy of the goddess Isis. Though emperors such as Antoninus lovingly cherished the antiquarian Italian cults, millions sought relief from the barren correctness of official worship in the oriental mystery religions—of Isis and Serapis from Egypt; Cybele the Earth-Mother and Attis from Asia Minor; Dionysus (Bacchus) from Thrace; and even more exotic deities. To the accompaniment of thrilling cult-dramas symbolising the growth and death of the year, these cults offered grades of initiation promising privilege in the after-life, with no distinction between persons or sexes.

Snake-god Sabazius; Atargatis half woman half fish

The terrifying ceremonial of Mithras, identified with the life-giving sun, added liturgy, baptism and sacramental meals. Its stern Iranian ethical code—associated with bloody bull sacrifices—attracted many throughout the western empire, including army officers. This was an age of superstitious credulity and hysteria, in contrast to, or provoked by, the placid materialism of daily life. Books interpreting dreams were best-sellers, and wandering seers were credited with miraculous healing powers. In particular, astrology had countless supporters. For most inhabitants of the empire believed that the planets and signs of the zodiac controlled their fate—and they sought to evade or influence this control.

Worshippers of Cybele bathed in the blood of bull or ram

Under Aurelius's son Commodus (180–92) this hankering for contact with heaven begins to become apparent even on the usually conservative coinage. Here we find a monotheistic Jupiter (accompanied by the seven planets) with the emperor as the divine Hercules, his regent on earth. Perhaps sensible in calling off his fathers's frontier expansion, the temperamental, megalomaniac Commodus was unwise in his rapidly changing choice of advisers. The last of these, with the emperor's ex-mistress, arranged his assassination.

Aurelius regrettably abandoned the adoptive principle

Rome was named "colony of Commodus". He fought in person as a gladiator

⟨ A.D. 150–192 ⟩

Caracalla
(nickname from
hooded Gallic
greatcoat)
murdered his
brother,
executed
outstanding
lawyer
Papinian (212)

Within a few months after the murder of Commodus, two more emperors had been acclaimed and murdered. The second of them,
Didius Julianus, had set a sinister precedent by
buying the throne by auction from the Guard.
The fierce, extremely capable Septimius Severus
(193–211) only asserted his claim against the
nominees of rival armies after four years of civil
war—as ruinous as the wars after Nero's death.
Severus embarked on ambitious plans. Repairing
frontier defences, he maintained aggressive foreign
policies, reoccupying Mesopotamia and invading
northern Scotland (209). These wars were defrayed
from rigorously extracted taxes—all the heavier
since in the calculations of Severus the legionaries
eclipsed the Senate, receiving pay increases of
over 30 per cent.

Severus was active in military road-building. He created three new legions

Commodus had already increased pay by 25%

Stability returned, but it was more careworn than that of the Antonine
Age which Severus claimed to revive. True to his north African origins
(his wife Julia Domna was a Syrian patroness of letters) he equated
Italians with provincials, from whom even the Guardsmen were now
drawn.

His restlessly neurotic, tyrannical son Caracalla (211–17), though
abandoning his father's plans in Britain, intensified his other policies
by a fresh 50 per cent army pay increase and the extension of Roman
citizenship to all free men within the borders of the empire. When
Caracalla's attempt to win eastern laurels ended in assassination, Rome
experienced the orgiastic despotism of his 14-year-old second cousin
Elagabalus (218–22). The murder of this priest of the Syrian sun-god
El Gabal was followed by a partial respite, during which his mild
brother Severus Alexander (222–35) and the empire were judiciously
ruled by a woman—the emperor's mother Julia Mamaea. But this
reign witnessed the threatening rise of the new Sassanian monarchy
in the East, more formidable than the Parthian which it superseded.

Franchise extension made all liable to death duty, now doubled

Sassanian Persians soon clashed with Rome

PART SIX
AFTER A.D. 235
FALL AND ETERNITY
OF ROME

Coin of Gordian II, A.D. 238,
"Eternal Rome"

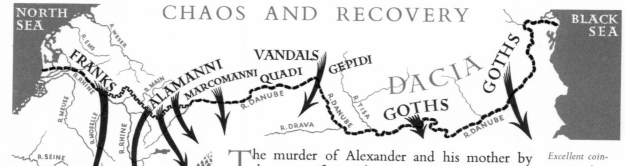

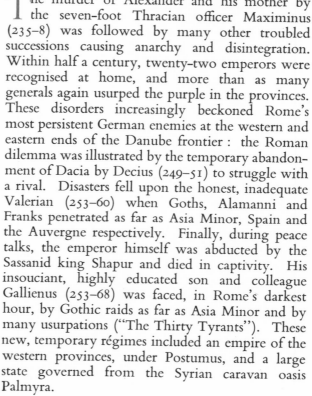

The murder of Alexander and his mother by the seven-foot Thracian officer Maximinus (235-8) was followed by many other troubled successions causing anarchy and disintegration. Within half a century, twenty-two emperors were recognised at home, and more than as many generals again usurped the purple in the provinces. These disorders increasingly beckoned Rome's most persistent German enemies at the western and eastern ends of the Danube frontier : the Roman dilemma was illustrated by the temporary abandonment of Dacia by Decius (249-51) to struggle with a rival. Disasters fell upon the honest, inadequate Valerian (253-60) when Goths, Alamanni and Franks penetrated as far as Asia Minor, Spain and the Auvergne respectively. Finally, during peace talks, the emperor himself was abducted by the Sassanid king Shapur and died in captivity. His insouciant, highly educated son and colleague Gallienus (253-68) was faced, in Rome's darkest hour, by Gothic raids as far as Asia Minor and by many usurpations ("The Thirty Tyrants"). These new, temporary régimes included an empire of the western provinces, under Postumus, and a large state governed from the Syrian caravan oasis Palmyra.

Inscribing his coins "Peace Everywhere", Gallienus began the long fight back. But Roman recovery, against all odds, was achieved by the almost superhuman military exertions of four army-appointed emperors of Illyrian birth (268-83). Claudius II "Gothicus" annihilated the Goths at Naissus (Niš) before dying of plague. Aurelian, "restorer of the world", evacuated Dacia permanently, but re-established the Danube line and broke the fourth Alamannic invasion. He defeated the learned Cleopatra-like Queen Zenobia (who, from Palmyra, had seized the eastern provinces) and in the same year (273) eliminated the empire of western Europe. Probus drove the Alamanni and Franks out of 70 towns they had captured ; and Carus pushed the Sassanians back beyond Ctesiphon.

Gallienus

Excellent coin-portraits show us the care-worn scowls and frowns of these rulers

Alamanni : displaced tribal groups. Goths : from Lower Vistula to Black Sea. Franks : combined relics of old German tribes. Saxons first appear in English Channel

Philhellene artistic renaissance under Gallienus, whose wife was patron of Neo-Platonist philosopher Plotinus

The Gothic threat was eliminated for a century

Aurelian built new Roman city wall

REFUGE FROM THIS WORLD

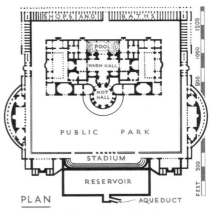

The Baths of Caracalla, Rome

Gaul and Rhineland lose trade. Mass production had not reduced the price of manufactured articles

In the towns of the empire it became increasingly difficult to find men willing to defray the extravagant expense of local office, and city institutions consequently decayed. Yet the eastern provinces did not share in the western "decline and fall" but survived the troubles of the third century, recovering from their relatively few invasions and maintaining or even extending their trade. Damage in the west was far more severe as insecurity became permanent The total area of cultivation and number of cultivators diminished—without compensating technical advances—and urban sites, except at pampered Rome, shrank with them as buildings were destroyed and industries collapsed.

Under Gallienus, "silver" coins are lightly silvered bronze. Gold was needed to subsidise barbarians

While insisting that their huge taxes should be paid in pure coin, bullion, or kind, the emperors continued to depreciate the silver currency and inflate its bulk. Consequently in the mid-third century a disastrous failure of confidence caused the whole economic system to collapse amid widespread misery and destitution. As extortion, confiscation and war decimated all but the very richest, land became concentrated in the hands of ever fewer proprietors, whose tenants now, by contract, became virtually serfs.

Empire could not afford high army pay, plus foreign and civil wars, plus bureaucracy (unpaid services of rentier class no longer obtainable)

350 miles of catacombs (Christian cemeteries) at Rome

Amid these conditions of crisis men turned to other-worldly beliefs for comfort. Christianity in particular, with its sympathy for the poor and for women and its gospel of kindliness, gradually drew ahead of other religions. Its organisation too was superior to theirs. In the previous century, with its untroubled communications, the Christian churches had compensated for their breach with the organised Jewish church by evolving a system of regular correspondence. Synods of bishops were also convened, and provision made for mutual financial support. Talented Christian writers in Latin now appear (e.g. the fierce African Tertullian) as well as in Greek. When, therefore, with the slogan of "back to old Roman observances", Decius and Valerian sought a scapegoat to distract the empire from its miseries, it was the Christians whose persecution they encouraged.

Gallienus rescinded the persecutions; Severus Alexander had accepted Abraham and Christ in his pantheon

61

〈 A.D. 235–284 〉

NEW ROME

Elaborate court ceremonial and etiquette (introduced by Aurelian with sun worship) foreshadowed Byzantium

The Illyrians Diocletian (284–305) and Constantine (306–37) reorganised the reunited empire, but the price its peoples paid for restored frontiers was a totalitarian state on eastern models, in perpetual crisis and inflation, with a corrupt, extortionate, omnicompetent bureaucracy.

An attempt by Diocletian to solve the succession problem by a "tetrarchy"—two reigning emperors and two emperors-designate (Caesars)—failed after his abdication ; and Constantine seized power.

Diocletian retired to Salonae (Split, Yugoslavia). His capital had been at Nicomedia (Izmit, NW. Asia Minor)

Two measures of Constantine heralded a new era. First, soon after a fresh wave of persecutions by his predecessors, he accepted Christianity (312) and accorded it freedom of worship, taking part in the Council of Nicaea (Iznik, NW. Asia Minor : 325) ; within a century the great Christian literature of Ambrose, Augustine, Jerome and Prudentius was to follow. Secondly, realising that Rome was no longer central or defensible from northern threats, Constantine reconstructed Byzantium as his new capital, New Rome or Constantinopolis.

Paganism, strong at Rome, temporarily restored by Julian "the Apostate" (361-3)

WESTERN EMPIRE   EASTERN EMPIRE

Constantine

Henceforward the empire, though theoretically united, was usually divided, with one ruler at Constantinople and one in Italy (at Ravenna or Milan). But the severance of the western provinces from the still rich and populous Eastern Mediterranean combined with internal dissensions to cause the gradual obliteration of their defences, and in the early fifth century they successively passed beyond imperial control. In 476 the last Roman emperor, Romulus "Augustulus", was quietly deposed by the German Odoacer, and Italy soon ceased to be within the empire.

Rome, sacked by Alaric the Goth in 410, gradually became depopulated

Terrifying Hun empire of Attila (d. 453) in N. Europe rose and fell

Justinian

The Byzantine régime lasted until 1453. Although becoming gradually Hellenised and orientalised, it continued to call itself the "empire of the Romans". The fifth and sixth centuries produced two outstanding monuments of Roman state-craft, the legal codes of Theodosius II and Justinian I (530–4).

Justinian I temporarily reconquered Italy (536-67)

⟨ A.D. 284–1453 ⟩

ETERNAL ROME

The Holy Roman Empire lasted until 1806

Symbolic of the survival of Rome's governmental ideas and traditions was Charlemagne's revival of the title of Roman emperor in Western Europe (800). He ordered the study of Latin, which persisted as the official and ecclesiastical medium as well as a popular tongue—gradually modifying into modern languages. Much of Rome's literature was preserved, Ovid the storyteller presiding over mediaeval poetry of Romantic Love while Virgil obtained a strange fame among the masses as magic wonder-worker. The study of these and other writers, at first kept alive in a few monasteries, gradually spread from the tenth century onwards. After *c.*1100 (age of the "Romanesque" arch) Roman law became prominent in the new Universities of Europe.

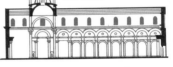

With the rise of an independent-minded, mercantile middle class in Italy, Petrarch (1304–74) gained inspiration from the belief in human potentialities displayed by Cicero—whose patriotic public life was admired by the next generation of Florentines. While the educators in this Italian Renaissance employed Quintilian, its playwrights drew upon Plautus and Terence, its architects studied the Augustan Vitruvius and the remains of Roman buildings, and its sculptors learnt from the busts, gems and tombs of antiquity.

Roman portrait

Donatello's "Niccolo da Uzzano"

SECTION

Church of S. Lorenzo, Florence

Renaissance sought inspiration from Latin and Greek writers. Rediscovered MSS included Cicero's Letters and some speeches

Though profoundly original, the buildings of Brunelleschi and sculpture of Donatello owed much to Rome, which they visited together in 1402 or 1405

Incessant discussions of freedom versus Caesarism. Machiavelli wrote on Livy (1515)

Burke, Gibbon, Robespierre and Jefferson were Ciceronians

The sixteenth century studied Tacitus. The Renaissance spirit now spread to France, Spain and—through Erasmus—to northern Europe including Britain, where Elizabeth I was an excellent Latinist. Milton's prose and poetry are both pervaded with Latinity, and Shakespeare—like the French dramatists—owed much to Ovid and Seneca. Latin remained the language of science until the late seventeenth century, and dominated English poetry, oratory and history in the eighteenth. The French and American revolutionaries were steeped in Cicero.

It was through Rome and its peace that Greek literature had survived and Christianity had struck roots, but Rome also provided its own mighty many-sided contribution. This has never been forgotten by any century before the twentieth—which will be the weaker if it severs itself from this great heritage.

In the 19th century Rome was mistakenly regarded as an inferior imitation of Greece

⟨ **A.D. 800–** ⟩